# FOUR STARS

# IN THE WINDOW

Tom Delvaux

EVEREADY PRESS
1817 Broadway • Nashville Tennessee 37203
615-327-9106

# ~ Dedication ~

*L*ike every young married couple, Harry and Eva Powell had no idea what the future would hold when they pledged to love and honor each other in 1919. Back then, the world seemed a safe enough place to start a family. The "War To End All Wars" had just ended in Europe. The peace had been won, and soon the Roaring Twenties would bring to America a booming economy and unrivaled prosperity.

And so Harry and Eva began a family, which eventually grew to seven children. But as they did, slowly the world changed.

First, a Great Depression plunged America into an economic collapse. And then madmen in Europe and Japan stoked the fires of hatred and conquest that ended in the conflagration known as World War II.

Through it all, Harry and Eva remained both a strength and a comfort to their children, true to each other and to their values. They supported their family, traveling the country to find work, making sure their children never went without. When their nation called their sons to war, they endured without complaint the agony of waiting for their safe return.

For their steadfast commitment to their family, for their unwavering faith and perseverance, for all the sacrifices they made for their children with gladness in their heart, we proudly dedicate this book to our parents, Harry and Eva Powell.

– The Powell Children

# ~ Foreword ~

## The History of the Service Star Flags

*D*isplay of the Service Star Banner first came about during World War I. During WWI and WWII most flags were hand made by mothers across the nation. One of the most famous flags was that of the five Sullivan brothers who all perished on the U.S.S. Juneau.

Each blue star on the flag represents a service member in active duty. A gold star is displayed if a service member is killed in action or dies in service. If several stars are displayed in one family the gold star takes the honor of being placed at the top.

Display of a Service Star Banner is done during times of war. Once again families are displaying banners at home. Banners may be purchased through the internet, at stores, or made by hand.

Additional information about the Service Star Flags can be found at...

http://www.bluestarmothers.org/flags.php

# ~ Contents ~

## Chapter One

# Behind the Stars

The flag hung in the front window of a modest home in West Hartford, Connecticut. It was a simple flag—four blue stars on a field of white, with a border of red—a sign to the neighbors, and to the world, of the sacrifice this American family was making, sending four sons—David, Kenneth, Delmar and Roger—into the military during World War II.

In many ways, the Powell family was not unlike millions of other American families of the time. The Blue Star Banner, as it was officially called, could be seen in the windows of countless homes, the blue star in many cases replaced by a gold one if the soldier was killed in service. (Many families, including the Powells, eventually chose not to display the banner on the recommendation of the government. Even in this time of overriding patriotism, the banner was a sign to thieves that the family was receiving government checks that could be stolen.) Indeed, there were few families who did not have a son or father who answered the call to defend their county. Immediately after December 7, long lines formed outside military recruiting stations. The rush was so overwhelming that one impatient youth, finding the line to join the Army too long, switched to the shorter Navy line. As a country of 130 million citizens, America mustered ten million men between the ages of 18 and 45 and another 30 million signed up for domestic duties.

And yet, few American families were subjected to the intense anxiety of having four sons involved in three different military branches—Army Air Corps, Navy and Marines. Fewer still faced the nerve-wracking uncertainty of having three sons fighting in three different military theaters of operation simultaneously. Consider, for example, the week of June 6 - 13, 1944. On the first day of that week, D-Day, one son raced across Omaha Beach to deliver medical supplies to the men. Two days later, another son arrived in England to begin serving as a B-17 co-pilot. Within six weeks, he would be shot down over Germany and taken prisoner. Five days later, a third son stormed the beaches of the island of Saipan in one of the most pivotal battles of the Pacific campaign. And a fourth son, soon to turn 18, had already joined the Army Air Corps and was awaiting his order to report to duty.

Ironically enough, the father of these fours sons was a Quaker. Born March 5, 1889, Harry Dale Powell was a farmer in Indiana for the first 30 years of his life. Even though most Quakers are conscientious objectors, Harry Powell was of a different mind. During World War I, he enlisted in the Army and was stationed at Fort Knox, Kentucky. Unfortunately, he contracted measles, which settled in his eyes almost blinding him (he had to wear glasses for the rest of his life).

After receiving his medical discharge, Harry met Eva Stoddard, a 25-year-old artist and schoolteacher. They married in 1919 and settled down in a small two-story home on 22nd Street in Marion, Indiana. Their first son, David Dale, named after King David, was born April 1, 1920. Fourteen months later, a second son, Kenneth Richard, named after Richard the Lionhearted, was born on June 20. Another boy, Delmar, was born on August 5, 1922. Four years elapsed before a fourth son, Roger, was born on June 22, 1926.

# Four West Hartford Brothers Of The Army—Navy—Marines

All four sons of Mr. and Mrs. H.D. Powell of Lancaster Road entered the service in 1942. (Reading top, left to right). Lt. Kenneth Powell, now home on a 60-day leave, was a prisoner of war in Germany for nearly a year. A pilot on a B-17, he was shot down over Germany in July of last year. Sgt. David Powell is with the Fourth Marine Division in the Pacific, and participated in the action at Tinian, Saipan and Iwo Jima. Delmar Powell, a veteran of the Normandy invasion on D-Day, has been assigned to an LST for duty in the Pacific, and Pvt. Roger Powell, the fourth brother, is taking pilot training in this country.  – *The Hartford Times*

In 1926, Harry and Eva decided to pick up their Indiana roots, leave the farm to the rest of the family, and make a fresh start in Texas. They settled in Dallas, but within a few months they loaded up their 1928 Dodge sedan and moved to Park Place, a suburb south of Houston, into a large two-story white house with a long porch.

Harry and a business partner decided to start a new business. They already had a name - The Columbia Institute of Music - and they planned to have music teachers in all of the big cities of Texas. For a year, the business thrived. Then the Depression came. Money for music lessons, a non-essential luxury for any middle-class family, suddenly disappeared, and The Columbia Institute of Music soon folded.

There were some real lessons in moral courage and integrity demonstrated by Harry and Eva during this period of time. One day Harry came home to tell Eva excitedly about a new company that was starting in the Houston area, and he had an interview scheduled for a new position. When he returned home the next day from the interview, he told Eva he had turned down the job. He explained it was a job delivering a new soft drink called "7-Up." The makers expected it to become a success because it would be used as a mixer with whiskey. This was 1933-Prohibition had been repealed. Harry said he just could not accept a job delivering something that would be used with whiskey. Now, here was a man with no job, no money, a wife and young children, and he refused a job because it would contribute to the use of alcohol. There was no relief program at this time, no food stamps, but he had the courage to stand by his convictions. Harry and Eva never gave up or forsook their faith. They read the Bible to their children and required them to say their prayers every night.

Once again, the family packed their bags and this time, headed to a farm 10 miles outside of Tampa, Florida, where Eva's parents lived. The Stoddards were living rent-free in a big farm house owned by wealthy people living in Canada. The Stoddards and the Powells took care of the farm's rabbits, chickens and 14 cows. There was a small lake and a stand of fruit trees, and the farm house had two wings separated by a large screened-in breezeway. While living there, the Powells had another son, Harry Jr., one daughter Kathleen, and the last of the seven children, Joseph William Powell (Billy Joe), who was born in January of 1935.

The Depression hit Tampa hard. Harry sold cars at a local dealership, but customers were few and sometimes the bills didn't get paid. When David and Ken completed their studies at Memorial Junior High in Tampa, their father bought them two new store-bought suits for the graduation ceremony. The two boys were proud of their new light gray suits, but after graduation, the suits disappeared. Delmar asked his mother what happened to the suits. "We had to return them," she simply replied.

Eventually, the older boys had to quit high school and go to work. David joined the Army. Delmar joined the CCC (Civilian Conservation Corps), and Ken drove a panel truck for the local cleaners. Earlier that same year, Harry Powell, alone moved to Hartford, Connecticut, for a better job at an Oldsmobile dealership. One day, he sold a Cadillac to a man, who mentioned that he worked at the Pratt & Whitney aircraft plant. He was in charge of the Production Engineering Department and said his division needed to hire artists. Harry told the man he had two sons who were skilled artists and immediately wrote home to Tampa and told Eva of the job possibilities. He also sent Kenneth and Delmar instructions on putting together samples of drawings so the man at Pratt & Whitney could judge their artistic ability. The two brothers put together a portfolio and mailed it to Hartford. In a few days, they received word that two jobs were waiting for them in Hartford. They didn't even ask about the pay. This was the Depression. A job was a job. Soon, the whole family moved to Hartford and into a large house on Highland Avenue.

They had lived in Indiana, Texas, Florida and Connecticut. They had survived the Great Depression. But in this new home, they encountered their greatest joys, and faced their deepest fears. With three and then four sons off to war for four long years, a mother, a father, three brothers and a sister offered, day and night, a simple prayer: that none of the blue stars turn gold.

# Chapter Two

# The Making of a Marine

At five-foot, nine inches tall, and weighing a scant 125 pounds, the 18-year-old David Powell was built like a rail post. He was so skinny, in fact, that when he went to the Marine recruiting station in Indianapolis in 1938, they told him he was one inch and forty pounds shy of the required height and weight. But with the nation still deep in a depression, and jobs still hard to come by, David was not to be deterred. He promptly walked next door to the Army recruiting station and signed up.

For the next year, David served in the 11th Infantry at Fort Benjamin Harrison, Indiana, as part of a tank outfit. Then, in November 1939, he received an administrative discharge. The reason for his short military stay was a lovely young brunette. Her name was Martha, but everyone called her Martie. The two were married on September 5, 1939, but the Army required that young privates such as David request permission before

7

they married. David was duly given his discharge papers. The couple moved back to Anderson, Indiana, where they lived with Martie's parents and David worked as a butcher in the local Kroger grocery store.

Their first son, Harry, was born on December 4, 1940. And then came Pearl Harbor. With her son barely a year old, Martie didn't want David to leave his family, and as a father, David would not have been immediately drafted. But David knew he had to serve his country. The family had moved back to Hartford by this time, and when David heard that his brother, Kenneth, had joined the Marines, he decided to forego the Army and sign up as a Leatherneck. But first, David had to have Martie give her written permission for him to join. The Marines were not in the

David and Martie at home

business of splitting up husbands and wives. Married men could not join the regular Marine Corps, so David enlisted in the Marine Corps Reserve and arrived in Paris Island, South Carolina for boot camp. Because of his previous experience in an Army tank unit, as well as his familiarity with weapons and military procedures, David advanced rapidly through the ranks, moving from PFC to Corporal to Sergeant and tank commander in just six months. By June 1943, his unit was moved from Camp Lejeune in North Carolina to the West Coast and joined the Fourth Tank Battalion, part of the Fourth Marine Division. First formed in World War II, the Fourth Marine Division was composed, with the exception of two officers, entirely of Reservists. The unit was completing its training and was scheduled to depart for the Pacific Theater on Christmas Day 1943. But before his departure, David took an emergency leave and traveled back to Anderson for an early Christmas present: the birth of his second son, David D. Powell, Jr., on December 17, 1943.

In January 1944 the 4th Marine Division sailed from San Diego. Their first stop involved practicing landings on an unknown beachhead, which they later learned was part of the Hawaiian Islands. These landing maneuvers involved launching the tanks from a Landing Ship Dock, (LSD), onto the beach. The LSD was specifically designed to transport loaded landing craft, amphibious vehicles and troops into an amphibious landing area through a stern gate that lowered into the sea. The practice maneuvers were soon completed. Now it was time for the real thing, time to set sail for the Japanese occupied Marshall Islands. Time for war.

## Chapter Three

# A Half-Inch Short

It was Thanksgiving Day 1933, and young Kenny Powell was feeling restless. He and his family had just finished their annual turkey feast and Kenny, like any typical 12-year-old boy, had had enough of sitting and eating with grown-ups. Quietly, he slipped away from the table and stepped outside. He soon spotted a friend who had ridden over and left his bicycle on the front porch.

"Can I ride your bike," asked Kenny.

"Sure," replied the friend.

Kenny picked up the bike and was soon rolling down a hill by a park, enjoying the double satisfaction of a full stomach and the freedom that is prized by every 12-year-old boy.

As he approached the bottom of the hill, Kenny noticed a car pulling a large four-wheel trailer, loaded heavily with furniture, coming down the other side of the hill. The trailer was swerving from side to side, becoming more violent and uncontrollable with each lurch. Kenny knew something bad was about to happen if he didn't do something fast. He pulled off the road onto the grass shoulder. He heard a loud "Bang" and then everything went black.

The next thing Kenny remembered was excruciating pain as a man, the driver of the car, tried to pick him up. The bike was a mangled lump of twisted steel, crushed underneath the trailer, which had crashed against a tree. Somehow, Kenny was still alive. But the pain was unbearable: his hip was broken at the ball and socket joint. With Kenny screaming in agony, the driver managed to place the boy in the back seat of his car and take him to the nearest hospital. When the hospital called the Powells to inform them about their son, Kenny's mother Eva couldn't believe it. He had only been gone a few minutes when she had ventured outside to look for her son and noticed that the bike was gone. The driver of the car had no money; indeed, he had been moving all his belongings because his house was in foreclosure. Harry Powell had no money or health insurance either. He could not pay the hospital, and so the hospital would not provide care. Young Kenny had to lie on a stretcher in the hallway of the hospital until his father arrived to take him to Shriner's Hospital in Houston, where arrangements had been made. As he waited for the ambulance, the doctors and nurses did nothing to relieve Kenny's pain.

For five months, Kenny was confined to a hospital bed with a series of ropes, weights and pulleys to make sure his leg set in the proper position before it was placed in a cast. Finally, he was sent home with a body cast that extended from the toes on his left foot to up under his arms at the shoulder and down to the right knee.

Nine years later, that near fatal meeting of bicycle and trailer again changed the course of Kenneth Powell's life. On December 7, 1941, dressed in his Sunday best and waiting to leave for Sunday school, Kenneth was listening to the radio, when the voice of President Roosevelt came on the air and announced the Japanese bombing of Pearl Harbor as well as his intention to go before Congress the next day and seek a declaration of war. Before Roosevelt had the opportunity to make his petition, Kenneth Powell had already signed up. Early the next morning, the 20-year-old drove to Fort Devens, Massachusetts, to enlist in the Marines. He passed the first physical, but the second found a disqualifying abnormality. The accident had left Kenny's left leg a half inch shorter than his right.

*Semper Fi* was not to be.

Kenneth could have continued to work as a draftsman at the Pratt & Whitney plant. But on the drive from Fort Devens back home to Hartford, he realized that was not an option. Kenneth wanted to fly, and his determination to do so became apparent during the next few months. Kenneth went to see a flight surgeon to determine if the shortness of his left leg would disqualify him from the Army Air Corps. The flight surgeon told him it would not. Unfortunately, joining the Army Air Corps was a very selective process, and Kenneth would have to wait and take a battery of examinations to see if he qualified. The delay did not sit well with Kenneth. Impatient and frustrated, he traveled to New York City to enlist in the Navy. But then, standing in a long line, his papers in hand, ready to sign, Kenneth got to thinking. The old dream of being a pilot resurrected in his mind. "I don't want to be in the Navy," Kenneth thought to himself. "I want to fly airplanes." Kenneth threw his enlistment papers in the trash can and took the first train home back to Hartford. For several months, he took on a series of odd jobs, waiting for his opportunity to join the Air Corps. But Uncle Sam was not so patient. Kenneth was drafted to serve as an Army Medic and sent to Camp Pickett, Virginia, for training.

Kenneth was deeply disappointed—his dream of flying with the Army Air Corps seemingly dashed. His father drove him to the Post Office in Hartford and Kenneth joined a line of draftees boarding a bus. When it was time to say good-bye, the two shook hands, and for the first and only time in his life, Kenneth saw tears in his father's eyes.

The first night he arrived at Camp Pickett, Kenneth went to see the commander of his company, Captain Familette, to find out how he could be transferred from the medics. The captain replied there were only two ways to be relieved of his current duty: join the Air Corps or become a paratrooper. Kenneth had no desire to jump out of a perfectly good airplane, but he still had hope of becoming a pilot. Captain Familette then told Kenneth he would have to pass a high school level examination in order to be accepted as a cadet, and if he failed the test, he would have to wait 30 days to retake the exam.

As he continued with his medic training during the day, Kenneth began studying for the Air Corps examination at night. It was a formidable challenge. Kenneth had dropped out of high school after only two weeks in the 10th grade in order to help support his family financially. Almost all of the soldiers taking the exam were college students. Many had college degrees. Day after day, following hours of daily medic training, Kenneth parked himself in the base library to study algebra, geometry and a host of other subjects that his 9th grade education had not covered. He took the test, and failed. Undeterred by his lack of success, Kenneth continued to study and then again took the test. Again he failed, and for another 30 days, he spent even more time in the library. Just as his medical company had completed its training and was about to be shipped overseas, Kenneth took the examination for a third time and passed—barely. He was going to be a pilot after all.

## Chapter Four

# The Man on the Bus

Every morning, Monday through Friday, the city bus lumbered through the streets and suburbs of Hartford. The dew was still fresh on the tidy lawns of the neighborhoods surrounding Highland Avenue, and the slant of the early morning sun dappled the roads with the shadows of trees. Every few blocks, as the air brakes sighed with a gentle squeak, the bus pulled over to the curbside, picked up another group of riders and then, with a throaty growl of the engine and a puff of black smoke, jerked slightly forward and rumbled on. Block after block, the ritual continued as the bus and its growing crew of working men and women journeyed eastward, gliding down a long incline to the city itself, insurance capital of the world, then crossing the Connecticut River into East Hartford before stopping at the bus line's most popular destination: the front gate of the Pratt & Whitney plant.

It was the spring of 1942, and few places in America better demonstrated the fact that the country was now at war than this particular industrial facility. Established in 1860 in East Hartford and still headquartered there, Pratt & Whitney found its first success manufacturing machine tools during the Civil War. Now, with the company one of America's largest aircraft engine manufacturers, the East Hartford factory buzzed with activity, fueled by the military's incessant demand for engines to propel its planes. Eventually, the company built or leased seven additional plants and employed 40,000 people, who built almost 130,000 engines for the Grumman Hellcat, the B-24 bomber, the Vought Corsair, the Curtiss Commando and a host of other World War II planes.

The bus was always crowded. The war effort had made gasoline a premium commodity and only a privileged few with fuel rationing coupons had full-time access to an automobile. For most people, the bus was the only form of transportation available.

But even during these demanding times, chivalry still prevailed. The men stood in the aisle to give the women and children a place to sit. One of those men, Delmar Powell, was feeling alone that spring morning. Only a few days ago, his brother Kenneth had quit his job with Pratt & Whitney in hopes of joining the Army Air Corps.

For many months, Delmar had enjoyed his brother's company during the daily commute to work. Before December 7, he and Kenneth had driven to the Pratt & Whitney plant in their gray-green 1928 Model A Ford sedan. When gas rationing began, they had ridden the bus together. They were "Tracers" at the plant; their job was to supply illustrations for the "Operations Book" that machinists used to make cuts on a block of iron. The book explained the exact angle and degree of each cut, which was illustrated with mathematical precision.

After only a few weeks on the job, however, the department head for production engineering called the two brothers into his office to tell them their jobs as "Tracers" had been discontinued. Advancing technology was the culprit: photographs could now be used to illustrate the operation sheets, and the cost efficiencies were so significant that their services were no longer required. Because of their satisfactory work, however, Kenneth and Delmar were offered the opportunity for on-the-job training as draftsman for the company, training that could earn them a permanent position at the plant.

But now, with Kenneth gone, Delmar stood alone in the aisle of the bus, his hand grasping a pole to keep his balance. Suddenly he felt the cold hard gaze of a man eyeing him with a look of pent-up scorn. Delmar had seen him before on the bus but did not know his name. The man kept staring and staring, without apology. Then he walked a couple of steps toward Delmar and announced in a clear, deliberate voice loud enough for all to hear, "I've got a kid over there fighting this war. What are you doing here sitting at home?"

Delmar didn't know what to say. As he tried to muster up some words to respond, he felt the accusing eyes of the passengers settle upon him. He could have told the man that he was serving his country, that his job as a draftsman at the Pratt & Whitney company was as important as any that the military might give him. But he bit his tongue and said nothing.

A few weeks later, another man again confronted Delmar on the bus. Enough was enough. With his two older brothers already serving in the military, this 19-year-old felt duty bound to sign up. Delmar talked that night to his parents, who understood his feelings and reluctantly agreed with his decision. With David in the Marines and Ken in the Army, they agreed to let Delmar enlist in the Navy for a minority cruise, a four-year tour of duty for those under 21 years of age.

Because of his work at the Pratt & Whitney plant contributed directly to the war effort, Delmar, like his brother Ken, was exempt from military service. He could have ridden out the war in the comfortable seclusion of a nine-to-five job. But he didn't.

On October 2, 1942, Delmar Powell enlisted in the United States Naval Reserve. During the next three years, he would traverse the world's two great oceans, swim in an Atlantic hurricane, ride out a Pacific typhoon and find himself smack dab in the middle of the greatest amphibious military landing the world has ever seen, running across a sandy shore littered with land mines and dead bodies to deliver medical supplies to his wounded fellow soldiers on Omaha Beach.

# Chapter Five

# Square Knot Admiral

The bus was crowded again, and the throaty, smoky growl of the diesel engine reminded Delmar of his frequent and familiar trips to the Pratt & Whitney plant. But this time, his fellow passengers were not the working people of Hartford, but young men from all across America—Nebraska farm boys, machinists from Michigan, high school drop-outs from New York—an amalgam of geography and education, economic and social classes, now unified by the adventure that lay before them: basic training

For the next six weeks, Uncle Sam would go about the business of transforming these civilians into sailors, turning Mama's little sweethearts into men. Thanks to years of experience, the military had fine tuned this transformation into an exact science, using a proven formula of drilling, instruction, physical challenge, tight discipline, low-grade fear and high-octane authority. As the bus drove through the main gates at the U.S. Naval Training Center in Chicago, Delmar and the other raw recruits heard, for the first time, a sampling of the sounds that would inform their new life for the next several weeks, not, in this case, the gruff, authoritative commands of a drill sergeant, but the taunts of the young sailors already stationed there. "You'll be sorry!" they chanted, in a zestful, almost welcoming way.

Fortunately Delmar found himself well prepared for the challenges, both physical and mental, of boot camp. In January 1940, at the age of 17, he had enlisted in the Civilian Conservation Corps, (CCC). This federal work program, established by President Franklin D. Roosevelt in 1933, employed young men in heavy construction work, mainly in National and State parks. Most of the CCC recruits were jobless teenagers, often from poor families. Indeed, only those whose family income did not exceed $500 were eligible to join.

The CCC was hard, physical work. As part of a four-man dynamite crew working in Perrine, Florida, just south of Miami, for example, Delmar swung a 12-pound sledge hammer all day to drive a steel bit into the hard, unyielding coral rock. When the hole was deep enough, it was filled with dynamite, and an explosion soon followed. Tons of coral rock was excavated in this primitive way, then transported to construct long jetties into the ocean. The men were building a large protected lagoon that became the centerpiece of Matheson Hammock County Park. (The jetty, completely destroyed by Hurricane Andrew in 1992, was rebuilt and today the park is the most popular in South Florida.)

Delmar earned a dollar a day, $30 a month, but received only $5 in cash. The rest was sent back home to support the family. But though the work was not particularly rewarding financially, it did have other benefits. Weighing in at a scant 115 before his CCC assignment, Delmar gained 30 pounds of muscle during his stay in Florida. His body became chiseled, tan, and hard as the rock he had worked on.

In the evenings during his time in Florida, Delmar took a course in First Aid, sponsored by the American Red Cross and taught by an Army doctor. As a result of this training, when Delmar signed up for a second tour of duty and was sent to Yosemite National Park in California, he was placed in charge of the Camp Infirmary. Working and sleeping in an 8-man tent, Delmar reported to an absentee U.S. Army Doctor, who visited the camp only once after a truck had crashed and rolled over, injuring many. Little did Delmar know that his decision to take this First Aid course in south Florida would later determine his destiny in the Navy.

His naval basic training had just commenced when Delmar was called into the Commander's office and informed that he had been promoted to "Square Knot Admiral." This new position of leadership came about after the Navy had discovered that Delmar had participated in a Junior ROTC program during his sophomore year at Hillsborough High School in Tampa. The training consisted of marching, drilling and learning the Manual of Arms with the 1903 30-06 Springfield rifle. Because of his training as a 16-year-old, Delmar was now placed in a position of authority over a company of 120 men. The designation "Square Knot Admiral" came from the shoulder patch that Delmar would now be required to wear, which featured a red chevron on a blue background. Above the chevron, embroidered in silver thread, was a square knot.

During basic training, one of the sailors in Delmar's unit refused to take a shower, and it wasn't long before he smelled pretty ripe. Some of the men pleaded with him to take a shower. He refused. Even when the company commander ordered him to take a shower, he refused. "In that case," said the commander, "I'll leave it up to the crew." They promptly grabbed the man, kicking and screaming, into the showers and then washed him all over with a Navy scrub brush and Octagon soap, a strong, lie-based laundry detergent that burns the skin. When the previously dirty, smelly sailor-to-be came out of the shower, his skin was a glowing pink. And from that moment forward, he never missed a shower.

Eva Powell

... *"But when he traveled to his next assignment, he dressed proudly in a uniform made by his mother, dyed perfectly in Navy blue. No one, not even a commanding officer, ever noticed."*

After six weeks of basic training, which included standing in a chow line four blocks long in sub-zero temperatures, the graduating seamen were given a 30-day leave before reporting to their next duty station. Because of the high volume of men surging into its ranks, the Navy had run out of uniforms, and Delmar had to travel home wearing "civvies," civilian clothes. But when he traveled to his next assignment, he dressed proudly in a uniform made by his mother, dyed perfectly in Navy blue. No one, not even a commanding officer, ever noticed.

Del's first Navy uniform was made by his mother before he was issued one by the Navy.

Sometime during Delmar's basic training, the Navy asked each recruit to fill out a form and list their top three choices for naval service. Delmar listed Submarine Corps in all three slots, but the Navy had other plans. Probably because of his CCC First Aid training and experience, Delmar was placed in the Medical Corps and reported to Portsmouth, Virginia on December 1, 1942.

After completing seven weeks of medical training, Delmar received orders to report to the U.S. Naval Hospital in Pensacola, Florida. Known as the "Cradle of Naval Aviation," and today home of the Blue Angels precision air team, the Naval Air Station at Pensacola served as the primary training ground for U.S. pilots during World War II, with as many as a 1,000 air cadets graduating each month. They were the lucky ones. The inherent dangers of naval aviation, coupled with the inexperience of the recruits, made crashes inevitable and death an all too frequent occurrence. Because of his medical training, Delmar was assigned the grisly duty of assisting with the autopsies performed on these trainees in the hospital morgue. Many of the deaths occurred when the rookie pilots practiced dive bombing. After descending at a steep angle and dropping their bomb payload, the pilot pulled back on the plane's stick control to pull up out the dive. This violent and sudden change in motion increased the G forces, or gravitational pull, on the pilot. Extreme G forces cause blood to rush out of the pilot's head, causing tunnel vision. Eventually, if enough G forces are applied, the pilot passes out and crashes. Extreme G forces can even cause damage to the heart valves. The autopsies performed with Delmar's assistance were the first to identify this phenomenon, and their findings were the initial step in the development of a pressure suit, still worn by fighter pilots today, which uses compressed air to force blood back into the head.

At Pensacola, Delmar's athletic skill came in handy on a couple of occasions. Some of the men bet Delmar that he couldn't climb a long rope that hung from the top of an airplane hanger. Knowing that he could, Delmar told the men, "Double your money and I'll try it without using my feet and legs." The men convinced that this was an impossible feat, would triple the bet, and Delmar would casually grab the rope and hoist himself hand over hand to the top of the hanger. The money was good, and Delmar only knew of one other sailor who could perform the same feat.

Even before he entered the service, Delmar was an accomplished swimmer. In high school, he swam the 440-yard and 880-yard races and could hold his breath for three minutes. In Pensacola several sailors who could not swim asked Delmar to take the swimming test for them so they could stay in the Navy. Delmar obliged, but he always worried what would happen if one of those sailors had to jump overboard without a life jacket from a sinking ship.

After six months of service at the Pensacola Naval Air Station and a promotion to Pharmacist Mate third class (PH.M. 3.c), Delmar headed westward on to his next duty station: a small hospital at the U.S. Naval Armed Guard Base in Algiers, located directly across the Mississippi River from New Orleans.

Working in the Naval Dispensary at the base involved almost every kind of nursing duty, including monitoring Psych Ward patients confined all night to a locked room. One night, a patient attacked Delmar, requiring his rescue by fellow Pharmacist mates after they heard the commotion.

The attack, as it turned out, was fortuitous. Delmar was transferred to surgery, where he soon discovered he was a natural in the operating room. Recently promoted to the rank of Pharmacist Mate second class, Delmar worked as a scrub nurse. Within two weeks, he was assisting surgeons during the operation, working primarily with the base's chief surgeon, Dr. H.R. Smith, a Commander in the United States Navy. The two soon became an efficient team. In fact, Delmar became so proficient in anticipating the next surgical instrument to be used that Dr. Smith simply held out his hand and Delmar would slap the handle of the next instrument neatly into his palm. The surgeon never had to utter a word or take his gaze away from the operation.

One night, Delmar and a buddy were riding a city bus, when a pair of eye-catching twin girls hopped on. They were standing in front of the two sailors when the bus made a sudden turn that made one of the twins lose her balance and fall in the lap of Delmar's buddy. The quick-thinking sailor put his arms around the girl and yelled to the bus driver, "Hey, do that again!" The crowded bus filled with laughter, and soon Delmar was dating the other twin, whose father was in charge of all the merchant shipping in the port of New Orleans. Out on a date one night with this girl, standing in line to buy theater tickets, Delmar suddenly had the sickening realization that he didn't have his wallet. Informing his date of his predicament, she offered a solution: run quickly to her home, just a few blocks away, and pick up some money. When they arrived at the house, however, the door was locked and nobody was home. Delmar's date, ever practical, told him to climb through a window and open the door from the inside. Just as Delmar was halfway through the window, car lights suddenly appeared in the driveway. The date quickly explained the situation to the arriving parents. They both cried out in laughter, and without hesitation, the father reached into his pocket, pulled out a wad of bills and told the young couple to go have a good time. They did.

During his tour in Algiers, Delmar was often on ambulance duty. One night at about 2 a.m., a call came in to pick up a second mate on a merchant ship anchored in the middle of the Mississippi River. Delmar drove the military ambulance down to the docks, crossed the river on a ferry, and then drove to another dock near the French Quarter. From there a small transport ship took him out to the merchant vessel, and Delmar climbed up a long ladder to the ship's weather deck. He was quickly escorted to the Officer's quarters, where he found a tall man, about six feet, four inches, lying unconscious on a bed. A quick survey revealed that the man was a diabetic. The man was either in insulin shock or suffering from a diabetic coma. Delmar knew he had to have an accurate diagnosis before helping the man. Treating a man for a diabetic coma when he is actually suffering from insulin shock can be deadly. Delmar told the captain of the ship that he would have to take the man ashore and get him to a hospital. One of the officers, also a big man, picked up the six-foot, four-inch patient and moved him to the deck using a Fireman's carry. Eventually the patient was put in the back of Delmar's ambulance, a large square-bodied Dodge with two large doors in the rear. Each door had a window about 18 inches wide and 30 inches high. Delmar was speeding down the road when he passed a beer wagon pulled by a team of horses and loaded with barrels and barrels of Jack's Beer, a local brewery. Almost immediately after passing the horse-and-cart, Delmar had to stop at a red light at Canal Street. (Military ambulance drivers had strict orders to obey the rules of the road.) As he was sitting at the stop light, minding his own business, Delmar suddenly heard the shattering sound of glass breaking. He looked back to discover one of the large windows broken out and his patient covered with glass. Then, just as abruptly, he heard the unmistakable sound of a horse neighing, and saw a horse's head sticking through the broken window. The incongruous sight so confounded Delmar, it took him a moment to realize that the Jack's Beer Wagon he had just passed had crashed into the back of the ambulance. Delmar jumped out of his seat and helped the driver pull the horse's head free. The driver was as drunk as an old coot! He was yelling uncontrollably at Delmar, telling him it was all his fault and that the police, the U.S. Navy and the president of Jack's Beer were all going to hear about Delmar's negligence. Delmar had no time for such buffoonery. He told the drunk to go ahead and report him and quickly jumped in the ambulance and sped away, but not before finding the driver's name and the name of his superior.

Delmar finally arrived at the hospital and had his patient admitted. Later he would learn that the medical staff had worked feverishly to pull the patient out of a diabetic coma. It had been a very close call. But the story wasn't over yet.

About three weeks after his run in with Jack's Beer Wagon, Delmar received a summons to report to the officer's quarters. There, he found a Naval lawyer who promptly informed Delmar that he was responsible for the broken window in the ambulance and that he owed the U.S. Navy a total of $10.00 to replace the window. Delmar asked the lawyer if he had read the report he had filed. The lawyer had not, but still insisted that Delmar pay for the window. Delmar had had enough. He told the lawyer in no uncertain terms that they could lock him up in the brig if they wanted to, but he was not going to pay the $10.00. Then Delmar promptly proceeded to walk out of the room without even being dismissed! The matter never came up again.

By now, Delmar's skill in the operating room had become so extraordinary, his superior, Commander Smith, urged him to consider becoming a surgeon. Smith even sent a letter of recommendation to the base commander asking that Delmar be admitted to Tulane University in preparation for medical school. But soon thereafter, the exigencies of war would shape for Delmar an altogether different fate.

When Delmar enlisted in the Navy, he had been engaged to a girl from Hartford. Except for two visits home on leave, Delmar and his fiancÈe had now been separated for almost a year when, on August 5, 1943, Delmar's 21st birthday, a letter arrived. The two had corresponded regularly during their forced separation, but the reading of this particular missive left Delmar feeling stunned, worthless and alone. It was the proverbial "Dear John" letter. She had met somebody else. No one knew how long the war would continue to separate them. And so on, and so on, and so on. It all became a blur of words. Nothing seemed to matter. And for a while, at least in Delmar's mind, nothing did.

A confluence of circumstances conspired to arrange what happened next. It was a perfect storm of heartbreak and alcohol: a sad sailor seeking solace in America's most famous party town, New Orleans, where the alcohol flowed as freely as the mighty river it overlooked. An older Chief Petty Officer, who no doubt had seen the sad look on Delmar's face on countless other sailors, quickly surmised the situation and took it upon himself to, as he said, "make a man" out of Delmar. The unlikely pair walked a mere block from the base before entering a bar, where the Chief Petty Officer promptly ordered up a Boilermaker with a Depth Charge, an appropriate drink for a lad in the Navy.

Delmar grasped the glass, briefly surveyed the strange concoction in his hand, a shot glass full of whiskey dropped into a mug of beer, and then did what he was told and consumed it without stopping. Down the hatch it went! Almost immediately Delmar knew he was in trouble. The room began to swirl. Delmar had met his match. The Chief Petty Officer hoisted the disabled young sailor on his shoulders and walked him back to the base. It was the first, and last, alcoholic drink that Delmar Powell would ever imbibe.

Brothers Kenneth and Delmar

# Chapter Six

# Earning His Wings

For an entire month, Kenneth Powell belonged to nobody. Having just passed the Air Corps examination, he was told to report to Nashville, Tennessee in 30 days on February 27, 1943 for aptitude tests. The medical company he had been assigned to had been shipped overseas. So for the month of February, Kenneth was unassigned. To pass the time, he hung out with a friend, Earl Smith, who worked as a baker, helping him bake pies (55 in one night) and cinnamon rolls for the soldiers still in training.

The two weeks in Nashville were dreary and wet. Kenneth easily handled the aptitude tests, but decided then and there that he would never live in Nashville. Years later, the city would be his home for 47 years.

Powell's next stop was pre-flight training at Maxwell Air Force Base outside of Montgomery, Alabama. The pressure to perform was intense. With his 9th grade education, Kenneth was now competing directly with cadets who had two years of college or more, studying everything from Morse Code (a minimum of 10 words a minute) and navigation to the mechanics of the airplane engine and how to fold and pack a parachute. Essentially, he was having to make up five or six years of academic work in just a few weeks.

The academics were not the only tightly disciplined part of Kenneth's daily regime. The physical training was strict as were the rules of behavior. Demerits, known as "gigs", were handed out on a routine basis for bad conduct, and some of the more misbehaving cadets received so many gigs they were drummed out of the Air Corps. Kenneth was determined not to be one of them, and during his term of service at Maxwell Field, he received only two gigs, and these were handed out for dubious reasons. Kenneth had hated his experience at his previous duty station in Camp Pickett, Virginia, with the 20-mile hikes and hot, muggy weather, and he wasn't averse to express his sentiments. Two upper classmen from Virginia heard Kenneth make a disparaging remark about their home state, and ordered the young cadet to stand in the corner and sing "Carry Me Back to Old Virginny," an African American folk song that had become the state song in 1940. The first two lines of the song:

*Carry me back to old Virginny,*

*There's where the cotton and the corn and 'tatoes grow.*

Kenneth, however, came up with his own more personal version of the lyrics:

*Carry me back to old Virginny,*

*Cause that's the only way you'll get me there.*

The two upper classmen were so infuriated by Kenneth's insolence that they each gave him a gig, the only two gigs that Kenneth ever received during his time at Fort Maxwell.

After successfully completing pre-flight training, Kenneth's next stop was primary training at Dorr Field in Arcadia, Florida. His training plane was the PT-17, a beautiful two-wing, open cockpit plane that was used for years after the war as a crop duster. Students training on the PT-17 occupied the front seat, while their instructors sat in the rear with identical controls. Kenneth's instructor was Mr. Preisler. After flying together for eight hours, the moment of transition arrived.

The two landed in a little field in rural Florida. Mr. Preisler exited the plane, turned to Kenneth and said, "Okay pal, you got it."

"You mean take it up by myself," replied Kenneth, feeling both stunned and exhilarated.

"You bet," answered Mr. Preisler.

Less than six months earlier, Kenneth Powell had a desk job drafting the designs of airplane engines. Now he was flying solo in the blue freedom of the sky. He was on top of the world, and the green Florida landscape lay below him like his own personal fiefdom. The flight only lasted a few minutes, but the effect could not have been more thrilling. Kenneth knew he had a knack for flying. During the next few weeks as his training continued, he would put the PT-17 through its paces, doing every maneuver he could think of, what the book said the plane could do, and more. In fact, Kenneth was so eager to push the limits of his plane that one day he actually flew it backwards. He pulled back on the stick until the PT-17 was climbing straight up toward heaven. Slowly, the engine would lose its fight against gravity and the plane would start to fall backwards. Kenneth then took his hands off the controls and let the front-heavy nose of the aircraft tip it forward and back to a normal flight.

Having mastered the PT-17, Kenneth's next stop was Greenville, Mississippi, for advanced training in a BT-13. This single engine plane, which featured a more powerful engine, two-way radio communication and landing flaps, was nicknamed the "Vibrator" by those who flew it. Kenneth continued to improve his flying skills, frequently practicing stunt maneuvers making cross-country navigation flights and gaining confidence. But the young pilot was soon to learn the unpredictable dangers of flying, especially when adequate preparations weren't taken. A carnival had arrived in Greenville, and Kenneth was keen on making sure he got back into town soon enough to see all the sights. It was standard procedure when flying the BT-13 to idle the engine and let the oil warm up before taxiing out to the runway. But Kenneth was in a hurry that day and eager to take off, get the flight in the books, and make haste to the carnival. He figured that taxiing out to the runway would give the oil plenty of opportunity to warm up.

He was wrong—almost, as it turned out, dead wrong. Kenneth taxied to the end of the runway, waited impatiently for the "Go" signal from the ground crew, gunned the motor, and took off. About 200 feet above the ground, the engine suddenly stopped. There was Kenneth, looking straight ahead at a motionless and therefore perfectly useless propeller. Lacking proper lubrication, the motor froze up. Instinct kicked in. He pushed the stick forward, sending the plane into a downward glide so he could maintain enough air speed to control the flight. Fortunately, the runway that Kenneth had used was the one runway on the entire base that had a clear field at the end and not houses or trees. Kenneth made a smooth landing on the green grass, stopping a mere 15 feet from a fence. He was safe! Almost immediately, a jeep came roaring across the field, and a full-bird colonel jumped out. Relieved to see that no one was hurt, he congratulated Kenneth on his successful forced landing, then turned his attention to the cause of the malfunction.

"What do you think the problem was," asked the colonel.

"I'm not sure, sir," Kenneth promptly replied. "All I know is that the oil needle is stuck way up in the red."

The colonel climbed up in the cockpit and sure enough, the needle was in the red. Kenneth's secret was safe, although he was sure the colonel gave some kind of talking to the mechanics.

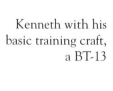
Kenneth with his basic training craft, a BT-13

After completing flight school in Greenville, it was on to Phase Three and twin-engine advanced training in an AT-10 at Freeman Field in Seymour, Indiana. Activated in December 1942, this Army Air Force Base trained over 4,000 twin-engine pilots on its four 5,500-foot runways during course of the war. Kenneth had badly wanted to fly the famous P-51 Mustang, a long-range single-seat fighter plane used primarily as a bomber escort. But because so many B-17 pilots were being lost in the skies over Europe, Kenneth was assigned to twin-engine advanced instruction rather than single engine. He reported to Freeman Field in Seymour, Indiana for training in an AT-10 that involved cross country navigation flying, night flying and navigating by instruments and radio. Kenneth had to learn to trust his instruments. Sometimes at dusk, with the horizon not clearly visible, pilots could not distinguish between the stars in the sky and the lights on the ground. He was tempted to turn the plane upside down, thinking his feelings might be right and the instruments wrong. Kenneth also learned to navigate by radio using the Morse code to fly "on the beam." A "dit" (a quick, sharp sound) followed by a "dah" (a long sound) meant you were "off the beam" to the left. On the other hand, hearing a "dah/dit", meant you were off course to the right. But when you heard single clear sound called "the beam," you knew you were on course.

Flying in winter weather was another challenge at Seymour. Kenneth often had to knock ice off the wings before he could fly. Many times he took off in a snowstorm, unable to see the end of the runway ten thousand feet away, and had to rely on his instruments.

The longer flights were often boring and Kenneth's co-pilot, lulled to sleep by the hum of the motors and the warmth of the cockpit, tended to doze off during these cross country excursions. On one such occasion, Kenneth thought he would have a little fun and break the monotony, so he gave a sudden shove forward on the wheel and then pulled back quickly to level off. The co-pilot lunged out of his seat and would have hit the ceiling if he had not been wearing a seat belt. He yelled out a cuss word, and he never went to sleep again.

At Seymour, Kenneth flew the AT-10. It wasn't designed as a stunt plane—until Kenneth, the original Top Gun, got in one. Once, in a hurry, Kenneth decided to forego the usual landing procedures: turning downwind, then crosswind and then making the final approach. "What the heck," thought Kenneth. "If I just gain an extra 1,000 feet of altitude above the runway, I can turn the plane upside down, reverse course and swoop down for a landing." He did just that, and with the plane hitting 350 mph (the AT-10s top speed was supposed to be a mere 160 mph), Kenneth swooped down and landed the plane. Fortunately, no superior officers saw the stunt.

Kenneth earned his instrument flight rating on December 2, 1943, an accomplishment that was well deserved. The weather was bad during this time of year. At times, flying in snow, Kenneth had to take off in almost zero visibility using his instruments to fly cross country from Seymour to Terre Haute and then to

Indianapolis and back. But he made it, and on January 7, 1944, Second Lieutenant Kenneth Powell, member of Class 44A, received his silver pilot wings at graduation ceremonies at Freeman Field. He was now a qualified pilot with an instrument rating. For Kenneth, the accomplishment brought an overwhelming sense of pride. For a boy who had not finished the 10th grade, he thought, he had more than held his own against his college-trained colleagues.

# Chapter Seven

# Top Secret

A 30-day leave is a prized possession for any young sailor. The restrictions and disciplines of military life are suddenly loosened, replaced by a freedom that is all the more exhilarating because it is so complete, and all the more satisfying because it has been earned.

When 21-year-old Delmar Powell received a 30-day leave in October 1943, he made a pilgrimage into his past. He first returned to Hartford to see his family, then took a train and journeyed to Park Place, Texas, south of Houston, to visit his childhood home at 34 Gulf Road. There, he visited the Reverend W.T. Turner and his wife and a host of other neighbors he had known nine years earlier as a teenager. Then, with a week left on his leave, he headed back to his duty station and explored the exotic city of New Orleans.

The 30-day leave had ended, but Delmar's wandering days were just beginning. A troop train, bound from New Orleans for San Francisco with 1,000 sailors, needed medical personnel to accompany the troops. Delmar got the assignment. These were soldiers headed to the Pacific Theater to fight the Japanese. The troop train arrived on Thanksgiving Day, 1943, and the citizens of the City by the Bay opened up their homes to give the soon departing sailors a proper Turkey Day celebration. Delmar sat down to real old-fashioned Thanksgiving Dinner, complete with turkey, gravy and all the trimmings served up by a family who lived in the country outside San Francisco. Unfortunately, the stay was short. Duty called, and the next day, Delmar was back on the train, traveling back through the deserts and mountains of the West to New Orleans.

The arrival in Algiers brought new orders. Delmar reported to the Commander's office thinking perhaps that his request to attend Tulane University had been approved. But it wasn't to be. A task force of medical personnel was being assembled for training in New York, and Delmar was to join it within the coming weeks. No one else was to know about his orders. As for the transfer to Tulane, the Commander had never gotten around to signing the order, which the top-secret mission would have preempted anyway.

In the middle of a mid-December night in 1943, Delmar Powell, gathered his gear and boarded a train that took him to New York City, then on to the Naval Training Station at Lido Beach, Long Island, where he joined, to his amazement, 3,000 other medical personnel. The instructions the group received were urgently clear. The group gathered here would constitute the greatest medical mission in the history of the United States Navy. The operation was TOP SECRET. Nothing about the operation was to be discussed with any outsiders, not even the mission's code name: FOXY-29.

In short, Delmar was now part of the United States Naval Amphibious Force for the Atlantic Theater of Operations. If the scale of the operation was immense, the implications were even more staggering; indeed, frightening. More than 3,000 men had been assigned to the specific task of treating soldiers wounded in one military operation. Delmar simply could not conceive of a battle with the magnitude to produce so many wounded. But no one knew that in just a few months, in the early morning hours of June 6, 1944, a fleet representing eight different navies, with 6,938 vessels: 1,213 warships, 4,125 transport vessels (landing ships and landing craft) and 1,600 support vessels, would cross the English Channel and begin the Battle of Normandy. It would be the greatest amphibious landing in the history of mankind, and the Navy knew that the number of casualties would be considerable. Because of a shortage of true hospital ships, the Navy had initiated a program to convert Landing Ship, Tanks (LST) into hospital ships to increase its capacity for treating wounded men.

By the end of the war, 36 LSTs were converted to serve as small hospital ships and designated LSTH.

During their stay at the Lido Beach Naval Training Station, Delmar and his fellow sailors received training in converting LSTs into hospital ships. Military training also continued. Marching and drills were conducted on a daily basis on the beaches of Long Island, and it was here that Delmar had his first brief taste of combat. Immediately off-shore from the drilling area was a naval target area. Navy airman would frequently fly overhead and fire their .50 caliber machine guns at the ocean targets. When the wind was right, the ejected cartridges would blow back toward land and drop on the marching soldiers, sometimes inflicting minor wounds.

As the sun rose on March 5, 1944, 3,000 Navy medics, having just enjoyed a light breakfast and dressed in their navy blues, picked up their battle packs and a newly issued carbine rifle, and boarded buses for a short trip to Pennsylvania Railroad Station in New York City. With specific instructions to speak to no one, the men silently disembarked from the buses, lined up in company formation and commenced marching three abreast in full-dress uniform, with weapons at right shoulder arms, down the city sidewalks of New York City. No drums. No bands. No cheers. Just the steady cadence of men marching, the heels clicking in unison on the sidewalk, could be heard, punctuated every eighth beat by the single "Hup" from Chief Petty Officers assigned to keep the march in order. A crowd of people formed, surprised by this intrusion, and stood silently, watching the young faces pass by. A few women sobbed softly; men stood at attention or held their right hand over their heart as a salute. No one said a word. It was as though America was holding her breath as her young boys marched off to war.

A caravan of buses awaited the men on the other side of the station, ready to take them to different ports, different ships, and different destinies. Delmar's bus traveled to New Jersey and the docks at Bayonne, and in the clear golden sunlight of an early morning, Delmar saw his new home: LST 508. She was clean and newly scrubbed, with a fresh coat of paint, battleship gray. Shortly afterward, with the gear stored and the men quartered, the LST passed the Statue of Liberty, and Delmar watched as the torch of Lady Liberty sank below the horizon and disappeared. Alone in the water, the ship sailed eastward to England and the coming invasion of Europe.

David Powell    Delmar Powell

\* \* \*

SGT. DAVID D. POWELL, son of Mr. and Mrs. H. D. Powell, 236 Laurel St., is on duty with a tank division of the Marine Corps on Saipan. He has also taken part in the campaign for the Marshall Islands. He enlisted in Aug., 1942, and received his previous training at Parris Island, S. C.; New River, N. C., and Camp Pendleton, Calif. He is married and has two sons. His brother DELMAR S. POWELL, a pharmacist's mate 2/c in the Navy, is now home on a 30-day leave, after participating in the invasion of France. He had been overseas since March of this year. After completing his boot training at the Great Lakes Naval Training Base, he was transferred to Portsmouth, Va., and from there to the Naval Hospital in Pensacolo, Fla. He then served in the operating room of the U. S. Naval Dispensary in Algiers, La. Prior to his enlistment in Sept., 1942, he was employed by Pratt & Whitney Aircraft. ROGER E. POWELL, 18, enlisted in the Army Air Corps and is awaiting call to active duty. Another brother, 2ND LT. KENNETH R. POWELL, has been missing in action over Germany since July 16.

\* \* \*

David on a visit to his parents' home

# Chapter Eight

# First To Fight

hen the Marine amphibious assault (code name "Burlesque") of the island of Roi began on February 1, 1944, a light rain was falling, and David Powell was listening to the radio.

The Pacific island of Roi-Namur is part of the Kwajalein Atoll, a group of 90 coral islets, 78 miles in length, that surround the third largest lagoon in the world. Roi-Namur is actually two islands, recently joined by a causeway built by the

Japanese occupying forces using Korean slave labor. The island was also the first combat objective for the 4th Marine Division, who arrived by ship on February 1, 1944. Marine tanks were transferred from cargo ships to landing craft (LCDs) that then made a ten-mile trip to a designated assembly area for the amphibious landing.

David Powell was listening to the crystal radio used by his tank crew to communicate with other tanks. The radio had the uncanny ability to pick up transmissions from nearby frequencies. In this case the aerial observers flying overhead were close to the frequencies being used by the tanks, and David and his crew could hear the pilots above reporting on the progress of the operation. In order to thwart any attempts by the Japanese to intercept their transmissions, the Marines employed an ingenious subterfuge. Different elements of the landing force had been assigned the different positions on a football team: quarterback, right guard, center, left end, etc. "The right guard is now progressing to the left and is being followed by the center, and the quarterback is fading back and throwing a pass." It was like listening to a radio broadcast of a football game, and of course, the Japanese had no clue as to what was being said.

When the Marines landed, Sergeant Powell was guarding the left flank as part of a company of light tanks, equipped with .37mm cannon in the turret, a .50 caliber machine gun and two .30 caliber machine guns. Almost as soon as they had hit the beach, their advance was stymied. Some of the tanks had been trapped by a Japanese tank ditch that traversed the length of the landing area. Finding this an unacceptable situation, Powell took quick action. He exited his tank and started walking down the beach to find a possible area suitable for crossing. He found a spot where artillery rounds had partially destroyed the ditch and made it passable. Powell quickly returned to his tank and drove over the makeshift bridge, followed by the other tanks in the platoon.

Japanese resistance was light on Roi, and six hours after landing, the island was declared secured. It was a different story on neighboring Namur Island. Unlike Roi, which had almost no vegetation because its airfield dominated the landscape, the island of Namur contained thick vegetation, and it took over 24 hours for the Marines to secure the island.

The 4th Marine Division set three new records in its capture of Roi-Namur:

- The first Division to go directly into combat from the States
- The first to capture Japanese mandated territory in the Pacific
- The Division also secured its objective in a shorter time than any other
- Allied operation in the Pacific since the attack on Pearl Harbor

.

David and his unit remained on the island throughout February 1944. But during their stay, an outbreak of dysentery forced the unit to be reassigned to the island of Maui, where they were quarantined for 30 days during the month of March. It was 30 days of rest and relaxation, the calm before the storm, for their next assignment was to be a fierce and hellish battle on the island of Saipan.

## Chapter Nine

# Life on the Home Front

Back home in Hartford, everyone in the Powell family was contributing their share to the war effort. Ten-year-old Kathleen Powell did her duty by stepping on and flattening empty tin cans before turning them in as salvage material. Kathleen also had the thankless job of mixing white oleo margarine with a yellow powder food coloring to make it look like butter. The oleo was hard and intractable and combining it with the food coloring was a hard job for a little girl. The father, Harry, rode a bicycle to work at the Colt Gun Factory, where he often worked two shifts as a supervisor for one of the most important war factories in the country. Eva, the mother, would keep the family spirits up by sitting at the piano and singing a song she had written, *Silver Moon on Your Journey*. When the air raid siren went off, the family huddled together in the dark, waiting for the All Clear signal. Gathering around the radio to hear the news of the day was a nightly ritual, and on many evenings, before saying good-night and going to bed, the family knelt in a circle of prayer, asking God to protect their three brothers and the millions of other servicemen who had left their homes to defend their country.

Soon, there would be a fourth star in the window. When war came to America in December 1941, Roger Powell was only 15 years old. He would not turn 18 until June 1944. Until then, he would continue his high school education. The fourth son of the family, Roger was perhaps the most athletic of the bunch. In the fall of 1943, he starred on the football team at William Hall High School in West Hartford. Because he was the most sure-handed of the defensive backs, Roger returned all the punts. In a game against Meriden, Roger took a punt on his team's 49-yard line, and thanks to some impressive blocking by his teammates, raced down the sideline for a touchdown.

On February 25, 1944, 17-year-old Roger Powell enlisted in the Army Air Corps as an air cadet for pilot training. Only four months later, when he turned 18, he would receive his orders. In the meantime, still attending high school, Roger and other cadets received training in assembling and disassembling a Pratt and Whitney radial engine.

On November 27, 1944, Roger entered the Army Air Corps at New Haven, Connecticut and was sent to Westover Air Force Base in Massachusetts.

There were now four stars in the window.

Although the average age of the high school senior is 17, a few boys have already reached their 18th birthday and are eligible for the Selective Service. Some of the Hall students who are in this minority have taken the foresight to apply for some special service of the Army. The most popular of these branches is the Army Air Corps, and recently a group of Hall seniors took the air corps test. Some of the boys went down to New Haven and were sworn into the Air Corps. However, they were told that they wouldn't be called to active service until they graduated from school. In some cases the boys took the test last year and now are receiving their notice to report to Fort Devens, from where they begin their Air Corps training.

Monday morning one of Hall's popular students was forced to leave school and prepare to go to Fort Devens on Tuesday. He was Roger Powell, who while at Hall was active in all school affairs, and played on the 1944 football team. Although Roger has left school for the Army, he will always be remembered by the students for the way he played his halfback position in the game against Meriden. Playing in place of the injured Bob Ducatt, Roger took a Meriden punt on his own 49 yard line, and raced down the sidelines for an amazing 50 yard run for a touchdown. The entire student body loses a good student and athlete to the Army, and everybody hopes that Roger may return soon to complete his high school education.

Roger Powell (kneeling right) with his crew

# Chapter Ten

# The Lucky Tooth

I t was March in the North Atlantic, still a wintry season, with none of the portents of spring. The weather was raw and cold and windy, and the color of the sea, a deep blue-black, seemed invulnerable to any warmth offered by the occasional rays of the sun. Along the rails of the LST, men slumped, their faces tinged green and their stomachs knotted with nausea. Almost no one was immune from the plight of seasickness. Being a flat-bottomed boat that only drafted seven feet of water, the LST could pull closely into a beach. But on the high seas, that design

caused a rough ride, and the LST would bounce up and down and slam against the waves, however small.

Standing guard at the snub-nosed bow of LST 508 at night, Delmar Powell felt miserably cold. Even though he wore special foul-weather gear and a thick mask made of felt covered his face, the clothing was designed not so much to keep him warm as to keep him from freezing to death. The frequent collision of the ship's bow and the sea's waves sent a spray skyward that landed on the front deck, then quickly froze, caking the guardrails and the deck as well as Delmar and the other guards in ice as they scanned the cold water for two potential dangers: icebergs and the periscopes of enemy submarines.

The trip across the Atlantic was slow and methodical. Originally designed as a beach landing vessel for tanks, the LST had a flat bow, which severely limited its speed to a mere six knots per hour. As a result, the sailors said that the abbreviation

LST stood for "Long, Slow Target," practicing the gallows humor common among fighting men. The crew's quarters on the ship were situated on the perimeter of the ship's hull, so that the guts of the ship consisted of one huge room, 248 feet long and 30 feet wide. The area, which had been originally designed to hold as many as 40 Sherman tanks, had been transformed into a giant infirmary, equipped and designed to care for hundreds of wounded. Soon after leaving the American coast, LST 508 joined a convoy of 60 other ships, protected by an escort of destroyers and cruisers.

The trip to England was not without its memorable moments. During his time with the CCC, Delmar had occasionally jumped into the ring on a Friday night and tried his hand at boxing. Just before Pearl Harbor, when David was home from the Marines, Delmar asked his brother to teach him some more pugilistic skills. The two brothers put on the gloves in the back yard and then David said, "Show me your stance." Delmar was looking down for just a split second as he was checking his position when—KABOOM!—he suddenly found himself sprawled out on the ground. All David said was, "Lesson #1: never let your opponent get set!" That vivid lesson came back to Delmar when one of the sailors on board wanted to box. The two sailors put on their gloves and Delmar nonchalantly said, "Show me your stance." Two quick left jabs and a right cross promptly followed and the surprised sailor was down on the deck. Looking down on his vanquished foe, Delmar repeated the lesson he had learned so well, "Never let your opponent get set." The sailor got up, took off his gloves and thanked Delmar for the lesson.

By now the convoy was sailing past the northern shore of Ireland, then dropped anchor at the Clyde River near Roseneath, Scotland, before traveling upriver to refuel near Glasgow. The convoy continued southward, along the western shore of England, rounding Land's End, the southwestern terminus of England, stopping along the way at a number of ports—Falmouth, Plymouth, Foey—to pick up and exchange supplies and men.

When these new men came on board, Delmar found a way to earn some easy money from them, just as he had in Pensacola, by announcing a challenge no one could resist. "I can chin myself 50 times with you hanging on my body," said Delmar, throwing down the gauntlet.

"You're nuts," the men would scream, to which Delmar casually replied, "Well, what's it worth to you?"

"We'll give you ten bucks if you can do it!"

So Delmar would hang on the bar, tell the gullible bettor to grab hold of his wrists, and start chinning himself without a single ounce of added weight. Oh, the money was good.

Upon arriving in England, Delmar received orders to transfer to the FOXY 29 group on board another ship, the LST 507. But that particular transfer never took place. Delmar came down with a bad toothache and was sent to the dentist before he could join the crew of the LST 507. That bad tooth turned out to be a lucky tooth, as well. For that next night,

LST 507 was sunk by German E-boats (similar to the American PT boat) during a torpedo attack in the English Channel.

The attack occurred during a major training dress rehearsal for the landing of the 4th Infantry Division at Utah Beach called Operation Tiger. On April, 28, 1944, sometime between 1:30 and 2:00 a.m., eight LSTs were heading towards Slapton Sands, England, on a clear, dark, moonless night. Two costly factors precipitated what happened next. First, only two ships were assigned to accompany the convoy: an outdated destroyer and a corvette. When the destroyer was damaged in a collision, it returned to port. Second, because of a typographical error in orders, the U.S. LSTs were on a radio frequency different from the corvette and the British naval headquarters ashore. When a British picket ship on patrol spotted two German torpedo boats on radar, the report reached the British corvette but not the LSTs. The corvette commander assumed the LSTs had the same information. It was a tragic mistake.

The first LST to take fire was 507. A direct torpedo hit engulfed the ship in flames, fueled by the gasoline on board. At about the same time, LST 531 was hit by a torpedo, and then LST 289 suffered the same fate. Five minutes later, LST 507 was hit by a second torpedo. Six minutes after it was hit, LST 531 keeled over and sank, trapping hundreds of men inside. Everything was happening so fast, there was almost no time to react. Indeed, only two of six lifeboats on LST 507 were lowered, and one of those, with a capacity of 40 to 60 men, was occupied by 80 to 100 men and consequently capsized. Enemy machine guns fired on the ships and on the men who had jumped in the water. Many of the men initially believed that the enemy fire was all part of the exercise, even to the point of yelling "Dry run!"

The other five LSTs were able to escape as LSTs 507 and 531 continued to burn and settle. LST 289 was able to make it back to port under its own power. When a British destroyer arrived on the scene at 4:00 a.m. to pick up survivors, LST 531 had sunk into the sea, and LST 507 had settled until only its bow was above water. It was ordered sunk.

Ten officers aboard the LSTs had been closely involved in the planning of the D-Day invasion. If any of the 10 had been taken prisoner by the Germans, the secrecy of the D-Day invasion was in danger of being compromised, possibly delaying the amphibious landing for months. Finally, the 10 officers were accounted for: all of them had been killed.

To keep the Germans from possibly learning about the impending Normandy Invasion, casualty figures were not released until after the D-day invasion: 198 sailors and 551 soldiers, a total of 749 dead, making Operation Tiger the most costly training incident involving U.S. forces during World War II. Most were trapped below deck and went down with their ships. Others leaped into the water, only to drown or be overcome by hypothermia in the cold water.

But for his lucky tooth, Delmar Powell would have been there and possibly not survived.

## SWEET SLUMBER

SWEET SLUMBER till dawn, till the last star is gone,
   I will hold you in my arms again tonight.
SWEET SLUMBER brings dreams while the moon softly beams,
   every moment brings a thrill of sweet delight.
I can see you in the shadows down a moon kissed blossom lane,
   there's a halo wrapped around us as long as dreams remain.
SWEET SLUMBER till dawn, till the last star is gone,
   nighty night until we meet again sweetheart.____SWEET heart.

Words and Music by AL J. NEIBURG, HENRI WOODE, LUCKY MILLINDER

## Chapter Eleven

# Flying The B-17

Kenneth Powell had five brothers growing up in Hartford. In Tampa, Florida, he laid claim to nine more. They were his brothers in arms, the nine men who would come together from all across America to MacDill Field outside of Tampa to train and eventually to fly into combat as the crew of a B-17 Flying Fortress.

Pilot:      Willie E. Johnson

Co-Pilot:      Kenneth Powell

Bombardier:      Joseph J. (Joe) Loverro

Navigator:      Raymond E. Malloy

Aerial Gunner:      Sgt. Paul J. Methfessel

Engineer:      Sgt. James D. Haire

Armorer Aerial Gunner:      Sgt. Leonard Rapoport

Ball Turret Gunner:      Sgt. Clair G. Gore

Radio Operator:      S/Sgt. John T. Murtha

Tail Gunner:      Cpl. Cletus D. Nolen

### The Crew of the Flying Fortress "Sweet Slumber"

*Photo taken at Turner Field, Savannah, Georgia the day the crew picked up Sweet Slumber*

*back row l to r:* Sgt. James B Haire / Engineer (Texas)
Sgt. Leonard Rapoport / Armorer Aerial Gunner (Pennsylvania)
Sgt. Clair G. Gore / Aerial Gunner (Michigan)
S/Sgt. John T. Murtha / Radio Operator (Pennsylvania)
Sgt. Paul J. Methfessel / Aerial Gunner (Wisconsin)
Cpl. Cletus D. Nolen / Tail Gunner (Tennessee)

*front row l to r:* 2nd Lt. Raymond E. Malloy / Navigator (Massachusetts)
2nd Lt. Willie E. Johnson / Pilot (South Carolina)
2nd Lt. Joseph J. Loverro / Bombardier (New York)
2nd Lt. Kenneth R. Powell / Co Pilot (Connecticut)

**401st Bomb Group 615th Squadron
Deenethorpe, England**

The crew represented a cross-section of America. Most of the men were single, but the pilot, Johnson, (the men always called each other by their last name) was married, had three kids and owned an oil business in Saluda, South Carolina. Loverro was a jovial happy fellow from Brooklyn and an excellent bombardier. Malloy could speak some French and believed fervently in evolution, a topic that he and Powell discussed on many occasions. Methfessel flew on 35 missions before the war ended. Haire was a tall, lanky fellow from Texas. Rapoport and Murtha were from Pennsylvania. Gore, a short, stocky fellow, was a perfect fit for the ball turret gunner, and Nolen, from Tennessee, was a tall redhead.

Their training began in January 1944 and continued until May. For five months, the men flew together six times a week, slowly learning to work as a single unit, forming the instinctive bonds of trust so necessary to function efficiently as a crew. Each man knew that he was dependent on all the others for his survival, as all the others were dependent on him. The crew practiced formation flying, aerial

Kenneth at home on leave, with Eva

gunnery, instrument flying and high altitude flying, wearing oxygen masks and leather fleece-lined coats, pants, gloves and hats in temperatures that reached 40 below. Bombing runs were practiced over and over; their target was Mullet Island just off shore from St. Petersburg. (Years later, Kenneth and his family camped at Mullet Island, which is now part of Fort De Soto Park.) The bonds formed during the training and subsequent combat were forged in the hottest fires and would last a lifetime.

In late May of 1944, the crew, having completed its initial phase of training, arrived in Savannah, Georgia, to pick up a shining, brand-new silver B-17G. Johnson named her "Sweet Slumber" after a popular blues song. Three days before Kenneth and his crew flew to Europe, he wrote his family a letter that concluded:

*I hope everyone is feeling as good as I am, being as good as Kathleen, and looking as good as Roger. Of course I realize that last part is a bit on the impossible side. No Remarks! I'm just building him up to suit the glamour of the Air Corps. Anyway Good Luck to you "Roge." Keep them babies flying, and the rest of you just keep on Singin, Smilin, and Prayin and soon we'll all be saying "Hello" instead of the usual...*

*Bye now!*

*Love Kenneth*

Now it was time to fly to Europe. First, they flew their new bomber to Bangor, Maine, then on the Gander, Newfoundland. From there they made a night crossing of the Atlantic to Preswick, Scotland, a long, seemingly interminable 13-hour flight. The weather was rainy and foggy in Preswick, but Johnson made a solid instrument landing and soon the crew was safely on the ground. From there, it was on to Stone, England to wait assignment to a particular bomber squadron.

## Chapter Twelve

# Strategic Bombing

There were two major purposes for aviation bombing of German targets. The first was general destruction and terror. The targets were population centers, especially those with large industrial areas. The British air force generally bombed at night without specific targets. The effect was what was important.

The Americans, on the other hand, flew daylight missions. Flying at an altitude of about 30,000 feet, with the famed Norton bombsight they were able to attack and destroy specific targets—buildings, air fields, rail yards—with strategic importance for the war effort.

Flying in broad daylight created very dangerous situations for the aircraft. The B-17 was designed to produce maximum destruction while providing all feasible protection for the planes and their crews. The nickname Flying Fortress was not just propaganda. Each airplane was fitted with guns front and back, top and bottom, and on each side. Flying in massive formations, often of hundreds and even thousands of planes, they were capable of filling the sky with machine gun fire in all directions. Nevertheless, losses were high, but the large numbers almost invariably overwhelmed the defenders, the anti-aircraft guns on the ground and the fighters in the air, and enough bombs reached their targets to make the missions tactical successes.

It was as a member of such a great formation of B-17s that *Sweet Slumber*, with Kenneth as co-pilot set out for the German heartland. The target for the day's mission was the railroad marshalling yard on the outskirts of the city of Munich.

# Chapter Thirteen

# Marshalling Yards

As the war in Germany progressed, it became more difficult for the Nazis to maintain their military activities. Three areas of increasing vulnerability were shortages of petroleum, especially for aircraft, tanks, and materiel transport; troop shortages and relocation; and general transportation within the nation, not only for war purposes, but also to supply food and other necessities to the population centers. The common link among all of these was the railroad system.

Flying almost six miles above the ground, it is virtually impossible to hit a moving train with bombs. They can be attacked by low flying fighters, but they were no real targets for the B-17s. Fortunately for the Allied air forces, it was necessary for the trains to come to a stop. Marshalling yards were large areas where train cars from different origins could be shuffled into position on trains heading for destinations all across the nation.

While they were in the yards, the trains were sitting ducks for the high flying bombers. Of particular importance to the Germans was the marshalling yards at Munich. Destruction of the Munich yards would destroy or disrupt rail transportation throughout the country.

Evidence of successful B-17 mission

Marshalling Yards at ULM

Photograph taken by 7th Photo Recon. Group, 8th Air Force.
Photograph provided by Marshall Williams.

The importance of these railyards was well-known to the German High Command. In preparation for the bombing raids they knew would be coming, orders had been given to move all available anti-aircraft (flak) guns to positions ringing the city. Also the remnants of the rapidly diminishing fighter force had been moved to fields in the surrounding area.

*Sweet Slumber* and its swarm of companions was headed into the teeth of the dragon.

It was June 6, 1944. As Powell listened to the reports of the D-Day invasion on the BBC radio, all he could hear was what the RAF was doing. Going outside, however, Powell looked up in the sky and all he saw were planes from the United States 8th Air Force. But listening to the radio, you would have thought the British did it all. Little did Kenneth know that a mere 200 miles away, his younger brother, Delmar, was looking death in the face.

Eisenhower talking to troops just before the D-Day invasion

## Chapter Fourteen

# D-Day

In early June 1944, southern England bristled with activity. For months millions of men had been waiting, cooped up in crowded bases. Tucked away in seaside ports, thousand of ships, including 233 LSTs, were standing by. Everyone knew the invasion of Europe was very near, and on the evening of June 4, when the First Army Headquarters arrived on LST 391, Delmar Powell knew the hour was close at hand. The men were called to their stations and poised for battle as the ship set out to sea, but out in the English Channel, a powerful storm turned the armada back to port. They would have to wait another day.

On the next evening, June 5, 1944, a convoy of ships, the likes of which the world had never seen and quite possibly will never see again, set forth from ports along the English coast and made their way to pre-assigned rendezvous points. As dawn broke on the morning of June 6, Delmar Powell saw his first sight of war: a U.S. Army Air Corps pilot floating face down in the water in his life jacket—dead. Everywhere he turned—bow and stern, starboard and port—there were ships, all headed in one direction, ships of every size, shape and function. It was an invasion force of such magnitude that it literally took Delmar's breath away. "How," he thought to himself, "did a kid from Hartford end up here in the middle of the greatest military force the world has ever seen?"

At 0600, aircraft by the thousands filled the slowly brightening sky. So many rounds were being fired by the AA batteries that it was literally raining steel as the discharged rounds of ammunition fell earthward, and for once, Delmar was thankful for his steel helmet. The three battleships assigned to soften up the enemy fortifications on Omaha Beach were now exchanging rounds with the German 88-millimeter guns. Feared by Allied soldiers and considered by many to be the most effective artillery piece on either side of World War II, the 88 was an extremely versatile weapon that could be used as an anti-tank gun, an anti-personnel gun or as an anti-aircraft artillery piece. Now an 88 was firing rounds just over Delmar's LST, which was positioned between two battleships. After a couple of near misses, the LST 391 commander got smart and moved his ship to a less threatened position.

Of the five Allied beachheads established that day, Omaha Beach was by far the toughest sledding. Within hours of the initial assault, the carnage was so extreme that the Army medics were out of medical supplies. LST 391 answered the call for help, loading a LCVP (Landing Craft Vehicle, Personnel) with supplies. A Chief Petty Officer asked for volunteers to carry the supplies onto the beach. Delmar, already in the LCVP, volunteered as did four of his fellow soldiers. When they landed, the five volunteers waded through the water amid a hellish concoction of smoke, noise and death. Soon Delmar was alone, carrying over 60 pounds of medical supplies and no weapon. He heard a small explosion under his foot and fell on his stomach, an act made almost instinctive by his training. Almost immediately, with his face buried in the sand, a loud explosion pummeled his ears and a concussive force shook his body. The initial small explosion was an anti-personnel mine sending up its main payload to waist level in order to maximize its effectiveness. A split second after the first explosion, the main charge ignited, throwing shrapnel horizontally in every direction with a force that would have cut Delmar into two if not for his quick reaction.

Somehow, when the blast cleared, Delmar picked himself up from the blood stained sand and continued on his mission. The beach was littered with anti-tank mines; indeed, an estimated four million had been placed on the six miles of Omaha Beach alone. Just as Delmar was about to step on one, he saw it, half buried in the sand, then stopped to mark the danger with a flag so the demolition experts could later remove it.

On he went, running through the closest thing to Hell that men can experience on earth: the deafening crash of cannon fire, the whistles of incoming artillery rounds crackling through the sky. The air was thick with black powder smoke and the choking exhaust of diesel and gasoline engines. Explosions far and near, the

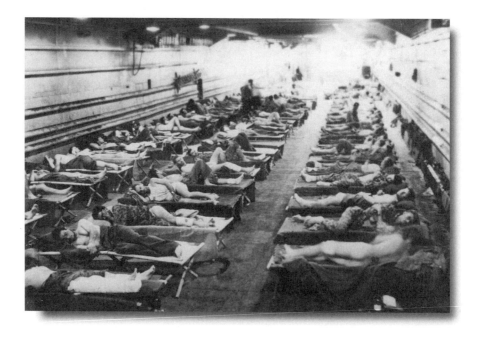

rat-a-tat-tat of small arms fire. For Delmar, the overall effect was as if a wall of steel was bearing down on him unrelenting and merciless at six hundred miles an hour. And then there were the bodies. American boys, so thick in places that Delmar had no choice but to use them as stepping stones. The sand in places had a red tinge from the blood of the 3,000 casualties strewn along the beach like driftwood.

Somehow the brave volunteers delivered the medical supplies and returned safely to the ship. Delmar was amazed that he was still alive.

The sights, the smells, the sounds of that day remained in Delmar's mind. Perhaps an excerpt from the official military report concerning Omaha Beach said it best:


"...within 10 minutes of the ramps being lowered, [the leading] company had become inert, leaderless and almost incapable of action. Every officer and sergeant had been killed or wounded... It had become a struggle for survival and rescue."


By June 8, D-Day plus two, the First Army headquarters had moved from LST 391 to the Normandy countryside and the ship unloaded its cargo of 40 Sherman tanks on the now secure beaches of Normandy. It was time for the medics to go to

LSI-6 Class

work. Like hundreds of other ships just like it, LST 391 became a working hospital ship, its now empty and immense Tank Deck transformed into a giant infirmary. The lesser wounded were placed in the upper troop decks. The more severely wounded were placed in the large Tank Deck. At the rear of the tank deck, Delmar set up his operating table, where he and 14 other Hospital men under his command worked non-stop. Delmar was one of the first medical personnel to see the wounded, dressing their wounds, wounds designed to kill, wounds that were filthy and bloody, some already oozing with infection, some still smoldering with the smell of burning flesh. It was a dirty job. On and on they came. The arrival of casualties was unrelenting. As soon as Delmar finished seeing one man, another wounded soldier was set before him. There was not even time to eat, so Delmar had a corpsman give him food as he continued his work. Delmar cared for 136 American soldiers as well as 36 German POWs, one of whom had to have his leg amputated. Not one of them died.

LST 391 had survived the initial bombardment from the German shore batteries during D-Day, but the ship was not so lucky when it returned to England with its tank deck filled with wounded soldiers. In the midst of a dense fog in the English Channel, it collided with LST 303. Though neither ship sank, both were extensively damaged, with the bow doors on LST 391 bent backwards. Finally, after helping unload the wounded, Delmar found a bed to lay his head down upon and slept for 24 hours. He had not sat down for two days and three nights. So traumatic were his experiences at Normandy that Delmar would not tell his wife he had been at Omaha Beach for 50 years.

# Chapter Fifteen

# The President's Prayer

On June 5, 1944, President Franklin D. Roosevelt announced in a national radio address that Allied forces had entered the city of Rome. The following evening, June 6, with British, Canadian and American forces still fighting forward on the beaches of Normandy, President Franklin D. Roosevelt again spoke to the nation by radio and asked his fellow countrymen to join him in prayer:

> *My Fellow Americans,*
>
> *Last night, when I spoke with you about the fall of Rome, I knew at that moment that troops of the United States and our Allies were crossing the Channel in another and greater operation. It has come to pass with success thus far.*
>
> *And so, in this poignant hour, I ask you to join with me in prayer…*
>
> *Almighty God,*
>
> *Our sons, pride of our nation, this day have set upon a mighty endeavor, a struggle to preserve our Republic, our religion, and our civilization, and to set free a suffering humanity.*
>
> *Lead them straight and true; give strength to their arms, stoutness to their hearts, steadfastness in their faith.*

*They will need Thy blessings. Their road will be long and hard. For the enemy is strong. He may hurl back our forces. Success may not come with rushing speed, but we shall return again and again; and we know that by Thy grace, and by the righteousness of our cause, our sons will triumph.*

*They will be sore tried, by night and by day, without rest – until the victory is won. The darkness will be rent by noise and flame. Men's souls will be shaken with the violences of war.*

*For these men are lately drawn from the ways of peace. They fight not for the lust of conquest. They fight to end conquest. They fight to liberate. They fight to let justice arise, and tolerance and goodwill among all Thy people. They yearn but for the end of battle, for their return to the haven of home.*

*Some will never return. Embrace these, Father, and receive them, Thy heroic servants, into Thy kingdom.*

*And for us at home – fathers, mothers, children, wives, sisters, and brothers of brave men overseas, whose thoughts and prayers are ever with them – help us, Almighty God, to rededicate ourselves in renewed faith in Thee in this hour of great sacrifice.*

*Many people have urged that I call the nation into a single day of special prayer. But because the road is long and the desire is great, I ask that our people devote themselves in a continuance of prayer. As we rise to each new day, and again when each day is spent, let words of prayer be on our lips, invoking Thy help to our efforts.*

*Give us strength, too – strength in our daily tasks, to redouble the contributions we make in the physical and the material support of our armed forces.*

*And let our hearts be stout, to wait out the long travail, to bear sorrows that may come, to impart our courage unto our sons wheresoever they may be.*

*And, O Lord, give us faith. Give us faith in Thee; faith in our sons; faith in each other; faith in our united crusade. Let not the keenness of our spirit ever be dulled. Let not the impacts of temporary events, of temporal matters of but fleeting moment – let not these deter us in our unconquerable purpose.*

*With Thy blessing, we shall prevail over the unholy forces of our enemy. Help us to conquer the apostles of greed and racial arrogances. Lead us to the saving of our country, and with our sister nations into a world unity that will spell a sure peace – a peace invulnerable to the schemings of unworthy men. And a peace that will let all of men live in freedom, reaping the just rewards of their honest toil.*

*Thy will be done, Almighty God.*

*Amen.*

## Chapter Sixteen

# The Battle of Saipan

I n early June 1944, operations in the Pacific theater stood at a crossroads. Up until this point, all of the territory captured by Allied forces—the Solomon Islands, the Gilbert Islands, the Marshall Islands and the Papuan peninsula of New Guinea—had only been recently occupied by the Japanese. Now Allied Forces were encountering the main enemy defensive line, heavily fortified territories that the Japanese had occupied since World War I. The fighting from now on would consistently be more brutal and bloody, beginning with the Mariana Islands and, more specifically, a 44-square-mile area of sandy beaches, rocky beaches and limestone formations called Saipan.

The capture of Saipan was critically

important within the overall strategic Allied plan of defeating the Japanese. With the atomic bomb still a work in progress, American strategists were still working under the long-standing premise that a successful termination of the war could only be achieved by a land-force invasion of the Japanese homeland. A vitally important first step in achieving this goal was establishing air bases that could begin systematic bombing of Japan. If Saipan came under Allied control, the island of Japan would then be within bombing range of the B-29 Superfortress. The new U.S. bomber, which was just beginning to be mass-produced in early 1944, had a round-trip flying range of 2,850 miles, more than enough to make the 1,200-mile trip from Saipan to Japan and back.

The battle of Saipan commenced on June 13, 1944. The armada of more than 500 Allied ships included seven American battleships and 11 destroyers that rocked the island with naval artillery. On the second day, eight more battleships, six heavy cruisers and five light cruisers arrived to contribute to the ongoing bombardment. The onslaught of firepower was phenomenal. A total of 180,000 shells were fired, including 16-inch rounds, launched by the big battleships, each weighing slightly more than a Volkswagen Beetle.

As the tremendous naval and aerial bombardment thundered above him, David Powell was working on the tanks that he would soon drive ashore into battle. During their stay on Maui, the unit had been issued used medium Army tanks. These tanks were loaded on the ships when the unit left Maui. The first time the Marines would operate these tanks would be in combat. On the way to Saipan, David and his fellow Marines would climb into the tanks and start the engines in order to keep the batteries charged.

The morning of June 15, 1944 dawned beautiful and serene. With the sun rising in the east over the island, the Marines landed on the western shore along 4 miles of beach called Chalan Kanoa. The landing of 8,000 Marines came under tremendous fire with 28 tanks destroyed the first day. The Japanese had positioned colored flags in the lagoon to mark the range of the landing force, allowing their howitzers, located behind Mount Fina Susu, to hit the advancing American forces with deadly accuracy. Somehow, David's platoon landed with no losses. Shortly after landing, the unit received orders to conduct an armored raid on Agingan Peninsula, about 2,500 yards to the south and located on the southwestern tip of the island. Once that area was secured, the unit was routed through a large cane field that had caught fire. The escape hatch at the bottom of David's tank fell off, and the crowded confines of the tank soon filled with smoke as flames darted through the open hatch. It was an uncomfortable but not overtly dangerous situation, and enemy opposition was light. As night began to fall, the crew was ordered to bivouac on the beach and as the Marines dug in, Japanese fighter planes suddenly appeared and strafed the beach with machine gun fire. They flew so close that David could see the pilots grinning through the cockpit glass.

By nightfall of the first day, the Marines had established a beachhead six miles wide and half a mile inland. The next morning the infantry resumed its attack in order to reach what was called the O-1 line, which ran along the first ridge east of the beaches. When they reached the top of the ridge, they encountered stiff resistance. At this juncture in the battle, David's platoon was still being held in reserve. David was called over by a lieutenant and ordered to take another tank, move up and join the company executive officer, Lieutenant Dollard, and reinforce the advance. The men on the top of the ridge were under heavy fire, reported to be coming from the edge of Aslito Airfield, located a few thousand yards to the southeast. When David and the other tanks reached the ridge, they too came under heavy fire. Shells were exploding everywhere. David saw a round destroy the turret on one tank. David's tank was firing at anything that looked like it might hide a gun near the airport. Unfortunately, the radio in the tank wasn't working, so the only way to communicate with other tanks was with flag signals. David got the signal to withdraw off the ridge. Now the tanks, thanks to a suggestion by the infantry, went around the flank to the end of the ridge. From this new vantage point, they could see the origin of the enemy fire: six anti-aircraft batteries arranged in a semi-circle on the slope opposite the ridge. The tanks advanced rapidly on the enemy position and the Japanese retreated into a cane field. Caught in the open, the enemy was easy prey for the tanks, and scores were killed by machine gun and tank fire. Others were simply run over when the tanks were ordered to knock down the cane field in order to create a field of fire for Allied machine guns.

The next day, the 27th Army Infantry Division captured the Aslito Airfield, facing little resistance. At the same time, the 4th Marine Division reached the east side of the island at Magicienne Bay, effectively cutting off the Japanese on the southern quarter of the island. The 27th Army Infantry was assigned the job of securing this area. The 4th Marine Division began moving up the east coast of the island. The 2nd Marine Division, which had initially established a beachhead north of the 4th Marine Division on the west coast, was moving up the west side of the island. The eventual objective for both Marine divisions was the Japanese stronghold on Mt. Tapochau, located in the very center of the island. The highest point on Saipan, with an elevation of 1,550 feet, Mt. Tapochau dominated the landscape and gave the Japanese a spectacular 360 degree view of the island.

It was slow going and heavy fighting as each Marine division slugged its way up the respective coasts. The thick tropical vegetation and rugged terrain combined to make transport difficult even for tanks. On several occasions, David was sent with two or three other men on reconnaissance missions to determine if the tanks could negotiate the terrain on their own or if engineering support was required. These missions required David and his men to venture two or three thousand yards behind enemy lines, but fortunately, they always managed to return. Day after day, as the Marines made slow but steady progress northward, the fighting increased in its ferocity. At one point, the combat was so fierce that David's tank platoon ran out of ammunition. David radioed headquarters to inform them of their plight and was ordered to return to an assembly area for re-arming. On the way back, he received another radio message from an infantry battalion commander on the edge of Magasini Bay, ordering them to his location. When David's tank platoon arrived, they found that their tank company commander as well as the rest of the company had also been ordered to the site. The Marines were about to attack Japanese forces on Kagman Peninsula that ran eastward and formed the northern shore of Magasini Bay. The goal was to reach a certain point on the peninsula by nightfall, but intelligence had reported the peninsula was heavily defended. The Marine infantry commander had decided to lead his attack with a wave of tanks, hoping to create a "shock effect" that would send the Japanese into retreat. When Powell pointed out that his platoon was out of ammunition, he was told to participate in the attack anyway. Fortunately, the Japanese position lacked heavy weapons and artillery, and the Marines rolled through the jungle and secured the Peninsula by nightfall.

The platoon of tanks returned to the battalion command post and was forced to park in the open. The lack of cover almost cost David his life. Just 4,000 yards away loomed Mt. Tapochau, still under Japanese control. From this commanding height, the Japanese could easily spot the stationary tanks and lock in their artillery. As David climbed up on the top of the turret, four artillery shells exploded right next to the tank. Pieces of dirt flew through the air, and the pure percussive power of the shells rocked David to the core. He felt like he had been hit in the head, not by one, but by hundreds of baseball bats simultaneously. Although he sustained no apparent injuries, the traumatizing force of the explosion was obvious to others. David managed to continue his duties of re-arming and servicing the tanks though his fellow Marines kept staring at him, noticing the shell-shocked look in his eye and his wobbly gait. After completing his work, David reported to the company commander, who promptly grounded him for three days. It was the only time during the war that David was injured.

The three days in the sick bay were, in a way, a blessing for David. The battle of Saipan was the most physically stressful that he experienced during his time in the Pacific. It was June, and the sun was nearing its yearly zenith and bearing down on the tropical island with relentless heat. The temperatures inside the noisy, claustrophobic confines of the tank often reached 120 degrees. At one point, the tank platoon was fighting on the front lines for 10 consecutive days and nights. Water was another issue. There was precious little of it available, and the water purification systems available were sub-standard and inadequate. Most of the time, the men couldn't bathe, couldn't wash, couldn't shave. Their unwashed clothes were filthy, dirty and greasy. The men applied their American ingenuity, but this time, it didn't work: washing their clothes in gasoline, a commodity that was in abundant supply, gave them clean garments but blistered their skin.

After David returned to combat duty, the Army's 27th Infantry Division moved in between the 2nd and 4th Marine divisions on June 21. David's tank platoon was given the assignment of protecting the left flank of the 27th as the unit fought its way north, east of Mt. Tapochau. Situated on a high ridge that ran down the middle of the island, David could see the 27th down below, in a place given the inauspicious name of Death Valley, with a cliff separating the two forces. Intelligence had received reports that the Japanese were planning a counterattack that night, and David and his men prepared for the assault. That night, the Japanese broke through the lines of the 27th at Death Valley and reached the artillery of the 2nd Marine Division. Only a point-blank artillery barrage stopped the counterattack. The next day, the 2nd Marine Division relieved the 27th. The 4th Marine Division, which had continued to slug its way eastward through the Kagman Peninsula, was ordered to swing left and recover the ground that the 27th had lost. David's tank platoon protected the extreme right flank of this movement.

The next day, moving the platoon into position for another attack required moving through a rocky bluff down a narrow roadway. David led a group of men down the ravine to determine if the passage was passable for tanks. At the bottom of the ravine, right in the middle of the road, they found an unexploded 16-inch U.S. Navy projectile, the largest and most powerful artillery shell in the naval arsenal. Initially, the problem posed by the armament seemed unsolvable. The shell was too big and heavy to move. If David called in the engineers to blow it, the resulting crater would make the road impassable. There was a large drainage ditch that ran alongside the road, big enough for the tanks, but the powerful vibrations of the big tank engines might cause the shell to explode. Still, the drainage ditch seemed the best solution, and fortunately, the tanks moved ahead without incident. As David and his men were completing their reconnaissance patrol, they reached level ground. Suddenly, about 200 yards away, a Japanese solider jumped up and started running furiously to the nearby beach. One of the men asked David if he wanted to shoot him, but David had seen enough of death. "No," David said. "Let him go. We'll get him tomorrow." The reconnaissance team returned to their tanks at the top of their cliff and reported their findings to headquarters.

The next morning turned into a bloodbath for the Japanese. The Marines drove them into the beach, where their only chance of escape was to turn northward into the fire of the northern flank, where the five tanks in David's tank platoon waited. All day long, it seemed, they came. The tank machine guns fired incessantly, and the barrels of the machine guns were so hot that they glowed red with heat. They burned out three machine gun barrels on all three machine guns and had to call twice for an ammunition truck to reload the unit. By the end of the day, the Japanese soldiers lay stacked on the beach like cord wood.

The unit was about to run out of ammunition for a third time, and David was calling for another ammunition truck when they received orders to report to the infantry battalion commander. When the tank reached the CO, and David opened the top hatch of the tank and started to climb down. He suddenly spied a frightening sight. There, attached to the top of the hatch, lay an unexploded Japanese anti-tank magnetic mine. Loaded with 1.5 pounds of TNT, with a fuse set at five or six seconds, this armor-piercing grenade had the power to blow the top off the tank. But that was only the first surprise that David saw. Laying across the engine compartment were two Bangalore torpedoes, a long piece of tubing filled with explosives. David was able to remove the Bangalore torpedoes and then called in explosive ordinance experts to remove the magnetic mine and destroy all of the weapons. For David, the odds that all three of the explosive devices had not detonated and severely damaged his tank and injured or possibly killed his men were incalculably small. They were one lucky crew.

For several more days, the battle of Saipan raged on, but David and his crew were not involved. By July 8, the Japanese were so desperate that they launched one of the largest banzai charges of the Pacific War. For more than 15 hours, wave upon wave of Japanese soldiers rushed the American forces, screaming "Banzai" (roughly translated "Long live!") as the Japanese officers brandished their swords in the air in this Eastern ritual of war that allowed its participants to avoid the dishonor of surrender. So thick was the human wave that the machine guns fired belt after belt of ammunition, swinging the barrels back and forth, back and forth, until the barrels were too hot to function

On the last day of the battle of Saipan, there occurred perhaps the most tragic and lamentable event of the entire campaign. When the Americans reached the northern end of Saipan, they discovered a huge crowd of local men, women, and children huddled in fear at the edge of the island's northern cliffs. Japanese propaganda had convinced the citizens of the island that capture by the Americans would lead to unspeakably cruel torture and maiming. Death was the only alternative. Loud speakers were brought and Saipan natives tried to convince the frightened crowd that surrender would be harmless, but their efforts proved fruitless. Hundreds of innocent civilians as well as most of the remaining Japanese soldiers jumped from the high cliffs in an act of mass suicide.

On July 9, organized resistance on Saipan ceased. The killing was over. Of the 71,034 U. S. troops that landed on Saipan, 3,100 were dead (twice the number killed on Guadalcanal) and 13,100 were wounded or missing in action. The Japanese losses were staggering. Of the 29,500 soldiers who unsuccessfully defended the island, only 2,100 were taken as prisoner. The rest were dead.

David Powell had survived. For the next few days, he and his tank platoon took a well deserved rest. But soon the work began again, getting their tanks back in shape for their next objective, which lay a mere 3.5 miles to the southwest, Tinian Island.

## Chapter Seventeen

# Three Missions

On June 10, 1944, Kenneth Powell and his B-17 crew members arrived in Deenethorpe, about 70 miles north-northwest of London, assigned to the 401st Bomber Group of the Eighth Air Force. Kenneth was shown to his quarters in a Quonset hut. On his bunk was a suitcase as well as clothes and uniforms.

Kenneth asked, "Whose are these?"

The answer rang like an alarm bell in Kenneth's mind.

"That's some stuff that belonged to a fellow who was shot down today," came the casual reply. "It's yours now—if you want it."

It was a wake-up call for Kenneth. He was sleeping in the bed of a man who only yesterday had found his rest there the previous night, just before he was shot out of the sky. He was going to war.

For a week, the crew settled in, and on July 9, a Sunday, Willie Johnson and Kenneth decided to ride bikes to a nearby church in Weldon and attend services. It was an old stone Anglican church, and there were only a few people in the congregation: mostly women, a few old men, children and no young men except

83

for the two Americans. Fifty years later, when Kenneth and his wife Kathleen returned to Deenethorpe and visited Weldon, they were surprised to see that same church adorned with stained glass windows that depicted B-17 planes in the clouds.

It didn't take long for the crew of the *Sweet Slumber* to be assigned their first mission: bombing a V-1 launch site just across the English Channel in France. Also known as a buzz bomb because of the noise created by its pulse engine during flight, the V-1 was an unmanned aerial torpedo, the first guided missile used in war. About 25 feet in length and launched from the ground by a steam-driven catapult, it resembled a small aircraft with a stovepipe mounted over its tail and no cockpit. More than 30,000 V-1 rockets were manufactured during the war. Most Allied fighters were too slow to catch and destroy the V-1 unless they gained air speed by diving at the target.

Instrument panel like the one in Sweet Slumber. Ken remembers, "The instrument panel was riddled and smoke was all over the place. The bullets were flying between Willie and me in the cockpit. Man, what a time!"

The horror of war was revealed to Kenneth on his first mission. Flying in formation toward France, Kenneth was looking at the plane to his right. The Plexiglas nose of the B-17 gave pilots the opportunity to survey the skies around them, and Kenneth could see the pilot and the co-pilot and the bombardier. Then, just as they crossed the coast of France, without warning, a violent explosion covered the insides of the Plexiglas in red ooze. Flak had hit the plane, and the blood from the now-dead bombardier had splattered the inside of the canopy.

The target for Kenneth's second mission was much farther away than the first. This time, the B-17 had to make a long and arduous 8-1/2 hour trek across the heart of the Third Reich to bomb the transportation and railway systems for the city of Munich in southern Germany. To meet the dietary demands of such an extended flight, the Army Air Corps issued, among other food stuffs, a Ration D Bar, a four-ounce hard block of dark brown chocolate, made by the Hershey Company and about the size of a bar of soap. By the end of the war, the Hershey plant was making 24 million of these ration bars a week. Powell loved the D bar. He put it on top of his instrument panel as something to look forward to when the mission was complete. On the way back home to England, with no German fighters to threaten them, Powell and Johnson would put the plane on automatic pilot, unwrap their D bars, sit back and chew on the bittersweet chocolate. Flying at 28,000 feet, with temperatures sometimes as low as 40 below zero (the temperature fell two degrees for every 1,000 feet of elevation gain), the D bar would become hard as a brick and Powell had to bite down hard to get a morsel. But he didn't care. Opening up a D bar as he looked down on the beautiful white cliffs of Dover meant that he and his crew were safe, and there was no better feeling in the world.

The next morning, the crew was to fly the same mission over Munich. They followed the standard routine: wake-up at 0300, followed by a brief breakfast of powdered eggs, sometimes supplemented by ham or Spam. Gaining altitude over the English Channel as they neared the coast of France, the crew noticed they were not receiving any oxygen. With a cruising altitude as high as 35,000 feet, oxygen was essential in the non-pressurized confines of the B-17. Indeed, a sustained stay above 10,000 feet could result in crew members passing out or experiencing severe altitude sickness, so they were required to use oxygen above that altitude. The mission was aborted, and when Kenneth returned to base, he received a few days of leave. The young second lieutenant took a train into London, where he stayed in a hotel on Piccadilly Circus and heard the buzz of a V-1 rocket land in a park only a block away. For the next few days, Kenneth was less a soldier than a sightseer, walking the streets of London, taking in the sights, and eating his meals in restaurants before reporting back to duty at Deenthorpe. Little did he know that this would be his last taste of civilized life for more than nine months.

On July 16, 1944, the crew of Kenneth's B-17 took off on their third and final mission. After breakfast, hundreds of B-17 crew members filed into a large hut for a mission briefing. There was a large map at the end of the hut, and the briefing officer revealed the mission target. Once again, it was Munich. The officer told the crews where to expect the heaviest flak. He also showed the location of the I.P. (Initial Point) of the bombing run, the point at which the pilot and co-pilot hand over the control of the plane to the bombardier. As was usually the case during these briefings, the officers were told they had a choice as to whether they carried their hand gun: a military issue Colt. 45. It was repeatedly pointed out that officers who were carrying a hand gun were more likely to be shot if they landed in enemy territory. Reason enough, thought Kenneth, not to take his.

The official report of Mission 110 reveals more details:

*Briefing was again very early, taking place for 36 crews at 0230 hrs. All 36 aircraft became airborne within 34 minutes, the final one being airborne at 0600 hrs.*

Wearing jackets, pants and boots made of fleece-lined leather to protect them from the cold of high-altitude flying, the crew boarded the plane. The enlisted men entered from the side door; the officers pulled themselves up from a hatch opening behind the bombardier. This was the fourth straight day that some 1,500 B-17s from England, as well as B-24s from Italy, had bombed the city, and the Germans

86

were ready for them. The crew was flying shorthanded that day: Methfessel, the aerial gunner, was sick and missed the mission. And so with only nine crew members, the B-17 joined the giant armada, in the air and headed southeast. The flight to the bomb site was uneventful, but as the plane approached the I.P., the sky began to fill with flak as if black flaming popcorn was popping in the sky. All around them, the German fighter planes were mixing it up with the P-51s, and bombers, victims of flak, were burning and falling out of the sky. As the plane began the bombing run, Johnson yelled back to the bombardier, "Okay, Loverro, you've got it." Using the Norden bombsight, Loverro was now flying the plane, keeping as straight and level as possible. All Willie and Kenneth could do was just sit there and listen to the gunners holler at each other on their throat mikes as the 13 .50 caliber machine guns shook the plane.

"Fighters coming in at six o'clock!"

"One at nine o'clock low! Get him, Gore!"

The bomb bay door opened and the howling sound of the wind blasted through the plane. Loverro released the bombs, and Kenneth felt the plane, now several thousand pounds lighter, lift as they fell.

But then, just a split second after Loverro yelled, "Bombs away!" German flak slammed into the right wing of the plane, knocking out both engines. The blast ripped through and damaged the bomb bay doors, and the second round of incendiary bombs wouldn't release through the tangle of debris and twisted steel. Now, it was all Johnson and Powell could do to keep the plane in the air. With the two right engines out, the two pilots had to mash the right pedal with all their strength to keep the plane from going into a spin. With their thigh muscles burning from the exertion, the two finally managed to  control the plane and engage the automatic pilot.

But their troubles were just beginning. With only two engines working, the B-17 did not have the required power to stay in formation. Slowly, it drifted back, away from the security of the main formation. Flying wounded and

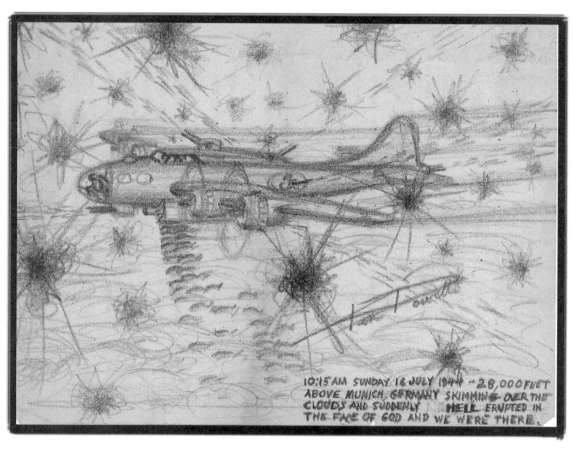

Within the drawing:
10:15 AM SUNDAY 16 JULY 1944 — 28,000 FEET
ABOVE MUNICH, GERMANY SKIMMING OVER THE
CLOUDS AND SUDDENLY     HELL ERUPTED IN
THE FACE OF GOD AND WE WERE THERE.

Drawing Kenneth made and kept on a bed slat at the foot of his prison bunk.

alone at 28,000 feet, they were now an easy target for German fighters. Before they could take the plane down into the clouds below, German Messerschmitt (ME)109s and Focke-Wulf (Fw) 190s circled in for the kill, like jackals surrounding their injured prey.

An Fw 190, also called a Butcher Bird, strafed the plane with its two 20 mm cannons. The shells tore into the top turret, where Haire was firing away, injuring and temporarily blinding the engineer. Nolen, the tail gunner, was also injured.

"Fighter ME 109, seven o'clock!" someone yelled out.

From the left rear, an ME 109 buzzed the plane, its .50 caliber machine guns blazing. The bullets careened through the cockpit, ripping up the instrument panel. When it was over, Johnson and Powell looked at each other, amazed that they were still alive, their hands doubled up over their chests. Powell was especially surprised since he never wore his flak jacket, which he considered too much of a cumbersome nuisance. What had saved them was a thick metal slab positioned behind their seats.

Chaos now reigned inside the plane. Smoke billowed everywhere. The crew's only hope was to use the power of the remaining two engines and their high altitude to half fly/half glide their way to neutral Switzerland. But that brief hope was soon snuffed out when the German fighter planes, smelling blood, made another run and shot out the two left engines. The plane was doomed. Johnson hit the "bail out" bell. Three short rings of the bell blasted through the plane. Everyone on board knew what it meant and immediately fastened their parachutes. The airmen were now going to test their skills as paratroopers. Johnson and Powell tried to keep the plane level, flying the plane like a giant glider as the other men abandoned ship. But with the plane losing air speed, it soon began to tip forward. Powell tried to make his way to the back of the plane to make sure everybody had gotten out, but the tangled wreckage around the bomb bay doors stopped his progress. Then he heard a shout from Johnson.

"Laverro and Malloy are gone," yelled the pilot. "Get out Powell so I can go."

With that, Powell put on his chute, stood next to the open hatch, looked down from 24,000 feet (the plane had already lost 4,000 feet from its initial altitude) and rolled out into the emptiness of space. There was only one thought on his mind: *"Shucks, I won't get to eat my D Bar!"*

POW memories painted by Kenneth, the artist, years later in art school.

## Chapter Eighteen

# Counting to Seventy-Nine

"One...two...three..."

Falling down through a bright and cloud-dappled German sky, second lieutenant Kenneth Powell was calculating when he should pull his rip cord. The trick was to wait long enough so that the parachute opened close to the ground, giving you less opportunity to be spotted by the enemy and a better chance to escape. Of course, if you waited too long, you'd become a permanent part of the German countryside, so it was a tricky calculation. Having bailed out 24,000 feet, Kenneth quickly figured he should count to 100.

"Seventeen...eighteen...nineteen..."

Now he was falling through milky white cumulus clouds, the type of clouds whose puffy shapes on a summer day inspire children to imagine there are fanciful creatures in the sky. But here, inside the cloud, having reached the terminal velocity of a falling object of 125 mph, it was a different story. Little raindrops, tiny pin pricks of moisture, repeatedly stung Kenneth's uncovered face. Still, he kept counting.

"Fifty-one...fifty-two...fifty-three..."

It was getting darker now inside the cloud. Kenneth wondered if he was closer to the ground than he thought.

"Sixth-eight...sixty-nine...seventy.."

Everything was turning black.

"Maybe I'm coming down on a mountain," thought Kenneth. "Maybe I need to pull the rip cord just to be sure."

"Seventy-eight...seventy-nine..."

Kenneth pulled the rip cord. The chute flew out and deployed with a quiet pop. Suddenly, instead of the sound of wind whipping his ears, all Kenneth could hear was a peaceful quiet, broken only occasionally by the sounds of bombs and war. Almost immediately, he broke out of the clouds and could see the ground, about 3,000 feet below. It was raining. Kenneth was coming straight down into the suburbs of Munich. To his left was a series of railroad lines, accompanied by a line of electrified high tension wires. To his right, Kenneth spotted a wooded area, so he pulled the rigging of his chute to guide his descent toward the trees, hoping the foliage would hide him and assist in his escape. But the wind was blowing him in the opposite direction, toward the power lines. The wind and Kenneth's steering cancelled each other out, and the second lieutenant fell straight down.

The ground was very close now. More than anything else, he was worried about the hip he had broken as a 12-year-old. How would it hold up during the landing? Would it have the strength to take the fall? Kenneth was not praying about his life. He knew it was in God's hands. But he was asking God to take care of him and to keep his leg from breaking again. His prayers were answered. Kenneth came straight down in the middle of large tree shaped like an open umbrella. As Kenneth dropped untouched through the maze of branches next to the trunk, the chute settled over the canopy of the tree, the shroud lines stretched and Kenneth came to a stop three feet from the ground, bobbing up and down like a kid on a pogo stick. As far as Kenneth was concerned, it was the softest landing in the history of parachuting.

He looked around and saw he was surrounded by 14 German civilians, each pointing a gun at him. There was no way to escape, and Kenneth was glad he had left his .45 caliber pistol back in England. If the Germans had seen that he was armed, they might have shot him on the spot. Kenneth was worried that they might kill him anyway. After all, he had just bombed their city, and he could tell that they were mad. No doubt everyone there had a friend or a relative who had been killed by the Allied bombing. Slowly, Kenneth unbuckled his chute and walked toward one of the civilians. The crowd grabbed him by the arms and took him into the basement of a nearby house, where Kenneth found, to his surprise, a cow as well as a big pile of cow manure and a long bench. A large heavy-set woman held Kenneth by the arm as the crowd discussed in angry tones what to do with their prisoner. Kenneth sensed that in their agitated mood, there was real possibility he might be shot. Fortunately, just as the discussion was reaching a fever pitch, two German soldiers, one from the Luftwaffe and one from the Wermacht, suddenly entered and laid claim to the prisoner. But soon the two soldiers entered into their own heated discussion as to who had the authority to take Kenneth prisoner. Finally, the Luftwaffe soldier won out. He was Air Force and Kenneth was Air Force, and that settled the argument. But even then, the civilians did not want to relinquish their newfound possession. The big German woman would not let go of Kenneth, and only after a considerable show of force did the Luftwaffe officer finally wrestle Kenneth away. He was glad he hadn't been left with the mob.

Aircraft 42-97982 was only on its third mission when it was shot down. Indeed, the plane had only been delivered to the 615th Squadron six days earlier. All nine crew members survived the crash and were taken in as POWs. The official MIA report read, in part:

*The members of the crew of Lt. Fred M. Taylor, pilot of aircraft 42-31863, IW-X, did observe at 1059 hrs, in the vicinity of 4820 – 0730, a B-17, apparently from the High Box of the 94th "A" C. B. wing, peel off and head back towards Switzerland.*

From the German side, the Luftwaffe report stated:

*Fortress downed by flak. Crashed at 1030 hours 10 kilometers southwest of Munich, at Neurid Forest Highway.*

Kenneth was put on a truck loaded with other American airmen who had been captured. Sixty B-17s had been shot down that day, and with a normal crew of 10, downed airmen were no doubt strewn across the suburbs of Munich. Kenneth recognized some of his fellow crew members in the truck, but there was no communication between them in order to avoid giving the Germans any information. The truck arrived at a small airport, and the men were ordered to disembark. A brief interrogation began. Kenneth didn't know what to expect. All he knew was that he was scarred stiff. After a few questions he was taken to a little room just wide enough for a bed and a small area to stand. Here, in solitary confinement, Kenneth spent the night. Looking out the bars of the window, he contemplated trying to make a run for it, but quickly gave up the idea. Escape, at least in this tightly controlled environment, was impossible.

The next morning, the POWs were gathered together and herded through the streets from the airport to a train station. As they walked through the Munich neighborhood, civilians threw rocks and debris at them. The train took the men to Frankfurt and then to a little town called Oberursel, where an interrogation camp was located. For two weeks, Kenneth stayed in the little camp, alone in small room. The routine was always the same. Every morning, a guard arrived and escorted Kenneth to the office of a German interrogation officer, Colonel Ulrich Haussman. The colonel asked a question and Kenneth's always answered, "Kenneth Powell, second lieutenant, 0820052."

As it turned out, the German colonel knew more about Deenthorpe and the 401st Bomber Group than Kenneth did. He even knew places in the States where Kenneth had trained. The young second lieutenant had been stationed at

Deenthorpe for only a few weeks and had flown only three missions. The colonel had had the entire war as well as scores of interrogations to serve as an information source. Kenneth sensed that the colonel knew that he didn't know much, so the interrogations were usually brief. He had heard rumors, of course, about what the Nazis might do to you if they suspected you knew valuable information, but the interrogation never escalated beyond the established routine. In a couple of weeks, Kenneth joined up with the three other officers of his B-17 crew: Laverro, Johnson and Malloy. The pilot, the co-pilot, the navigator and the bombardier were put on board a train bound for Barth, Germany, located near the Baltic Sea about 100 miles northwest of Berlin. The 300-mile trip, which normally would have taken no more than a day, took four because the Allied air raids had so decimated the German railroad system. During the trip, the train stopped for one night in the marshalling yards in Berlin. The Germans would often park prisoner trains in railroad yards in hopes of discouraging Allied bombing. That night, Kenneth and his fellow B-17 buddies heard the snarling roar of the RAF Mosquito and its two Rolls Royce Merlin engines flying overhead, and then, gratefully, heard it ebb away into the night.

Then, in early August 1944, Kenneth Powell arrived at what would be his home for the next nine months until the end of the war: Stalag 1.

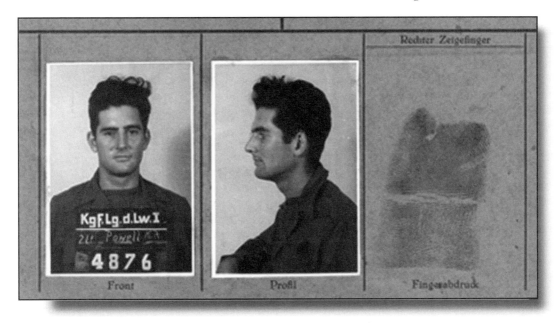

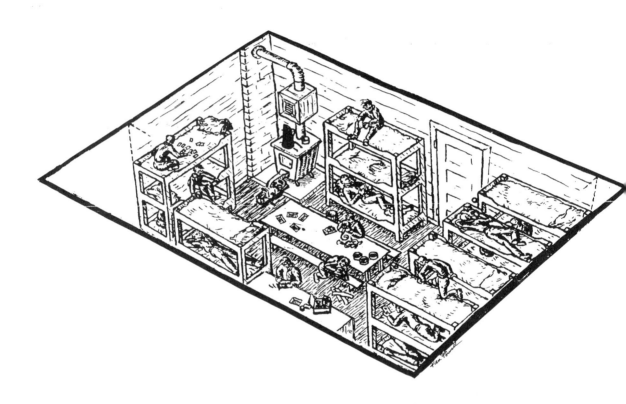

Ken's drawing of the prison barrack at Stalag Luft 1.

# Chapter Ninteen

# A Brief Reprieve

Delmar felt right at home, like he was back at a CCC camp in California. With his LST unfit for duty due to its collision in the English Channel, Delmar had been assigned to an R&R (Rest and Recreation) camp, a temporary station for the hundreds of D-Day veterans who had survived the Normandy invasion but had been taken out of action by a lack of equipment. The tent camp was home to 400 soldiers, who had nothing to do but wait until their new assignment orders were issued.

Four days later, Delmar received orders to return to the United States. He boarded a train that first stopped in Cardiff, Wales, and then headed up the west coast of England. When the train arrived in Liverpool, the troops had an hour layover, so Delmar joined a group who disembarked to explore this British city. The trip was uneventful until, on their way back to the train, the men passed by a pub and decided to go inside. The Yanks were greeted as royalty, like conquering heroes by the Brits, who were so thankful that these Americans had joined them in their fight to save their tiny, green island. So great was their appreciation that they refused to let the group leave until each of the men had downed a complimentary shot of Scotch Whiskey. After his initial encounter with alcohol in New Orleans following the receipt of his "Dear John" letter, Delmar had strictly abstained from adult beverages, but in this case he made an exception in order to facilitate the group's escape. The detour into the pub was unexpectedly long, and now the men were running to make it back in time to the departing train. They all made it—barely—piling on board as the train pulled away. It seemed to Delmar that the train's engineer, seeing the men's predicament, took pity and slowed the engine down a bit to help. With everyone on board, the train gathered speed, and Delmar fell into another deep sleep as the train journeyed through England's countryside and made its way to Scotland. There, Delmar boarded the USS Albemarle, a seaplane tender. A precursor of the modern aircraft carrier, the ship had hangars for storing aircraft, but no flight deck. Instead, cranes were used to lower the aircraft into the sea for takeoff and to recover them after landing. On the morning of July 6, Delmar headed westward, homeward bound.

Delmar was never one to indulge in inactivity, so when he saw a work detail list posted on the bulkhead next to the hatchway leading to the mess hall, he carefully examined the long listing of different jobs and signed up to paint the bilge. His buddies scoffed at the idea and thought Delmar was a fool. "We're survivors," they said. "That's how we're listed. We've fought in the war. We've paid our dues. We're just passengers. It's up to the ship's crew to do the work." Convinced of their privileged position, most of Delmar's friends didn't sign up for any work—until that evening, when you were allowed in for mess only when your name was called from the work roster! By the next morning, the work roster was filled with names, and by the time the USS Albemarle tied up in the Boston Navy Yard, she had been scrubbed and painted from stem to stern, the cleanest, best looking ship in the U.S. Navy.

Delmar had another, more crafty reason for volunteering to paint the bilge, the compartment at the bottom of ship's hull where water collects to be pumped out. At 500 feet long with a narrow beam and a deep keel, the Albemarle could slice through a calm sea like a hot knife through soft butter. But it was a bit of a different story when encountering the swales of the North Atlantic. Steaming through the continuous rise and fall of the water, the Albemarle produced a ceaseless long, slow pitch and roll. Delmar had begun to feel squeamish, but he found an answer on the work roster. By working all day in the very bottom of the boat, Delmar found himself in the ship's most stable area, while many of his friends worked above board and spent many hours leaning over the side rails, green, both literally and metaphorically for their friend below.

Arriving at the Boston Navy Yard, all of the survivors were given a 30-day leave, and Delmar made his way home to Hartford. For the next month, he mostly forgot about the war and felt both happy and grateful to be with his family. He talked a bit with his mother and father about D-Day his other war experiences, but for the most part, he preferred not to. The moments of horror were still too fresh and raw to be remembered. Instead, Delmar spent time with his brothers and sisters. There was Roger, now 17, the natural athlete of the family. Having enlisted in the Army Air Corps, Roger was waiting for his orders and practicing for the upcoming football season. Nine-year-old Bill, who was just beginning to show an interest in games like football and baseball, always wanted to play with his bigger-than-life brother. Harry, who turned 15 on August 2, accompanied Delmar on trips into town. Wanting to prove his manhood as 15-year-olds typically do, Harry taunted Delmar one night, mocking some of the judo tricks that Delmar had been taught as part of his military training. Sitting at the dinner table, Harry was pretending to be what would later be described as a "Kung-Fu" fighter, making exaggerated motions of a martial arts fighter, when Delmar, standing behind him and having had enough of this juvenile activity, suddenly said, "Oh yeah?" as he put his hand on the back of Harry's neck and squeezed slightly. Harry fainted almost immediately and his face fell into his dinner plate. That was the end of the mimicry.

Kathleen, the only sister in the family of five boys, was now 11. She had a cat. One morning, as Delmar was sleeping, the cat jumped silently into bed and proceeded to dig its claws into Delmar's thigh. He was so startled from his sound sleep that he instinctively grabbed the cat and flung it across the room. Unfortunately, the window was open and Delmar's throw of the animal could not have been a more perfect strike. The cat sailed through with uncanny—albeit unintentional—accuracy. Even more alarming was the fact that it was a second-story window. The cat was unharmed by the incident, but he didn't come around very much after that.

The family had recently moved to a house on Laurel Street in Hartford, just a block or so from the Colt Firearms Company, where Harry Powell was working. Roger remembers his Dad working all day and then working most of the night at the Colt factory where they made weapons for the war. Harry was not a young man then. Roger's most vivid memory is a conversation he had with his father as he was watching his father leaving for work at Colt. Their house had a glassed in porch and a glass front door. The fire burning in the fireplace could be seen from the street. Roger's father told him that leaving the house in bitter cold and snow, already tired from a days work, looking back at the fire in the fireplace and having to leave it was the hardest thing he ever had to do.

On a fair morning in late July 1944, Eva Powell received something in the mail that every mother and father whose sons were serving in the military feared: a Western Union telegram. In precise, official terms, the telegram stated that Second Lieutenant Kenneth Powell was missing in action, his B-17 having been shot down over Munich, Germany. The telegram was delivered by a messenger. Eva gave Delmar the telegram and asked him to go to the Colt factory and tell his father that he needed to come home. When Delmar arrived at the factory gates, the guard initially would not let him enter. Frustrated, Delmar demanded that the guard make a few calls.  Finally, father and son met and Delmar showed him the telegram and simply said, "Mom is asking for you."

## Chapter Twenty

# Matthew 6:6

It was, it seemed, just another ordinary day for Billy Joe Powell. School was over. Arriving home, he headed straight to the refrigerator for a snack as he called out, "Hi, Mom!"

There was no answer.

"That's strange," Billy Joe thought to himself. He called out again for his mother.

No answer.

The nine-year-old found his mother kneeling in a hallway closet.

"What's wrong?" asked Billy Joe. "Why are you in the closet?"

His mother answered as she held up a yellow piece of paper. "We got a telegram today that says your brother, Kenneth, was shot down over Germany and now he's missing in action."

Billy Joe said nothing.

"He could be dead," said Mother. "But I believe he is alive. I've been in the closet praying and asking God to take care of him." She remembered the verse–

*But thou, when thou prayest, enter into thy closet, and when thou hast shut thy door, pray to thy Father which is in secret; and thy Father which seeth in secret shall reward thee openly.* — Matthew 6:6

In just a few minutes, Delmar and his father Harry arrived. Husband and wife embraced and Eva opened her Bible. Her eyes fell on Psalm 34:20: "He keepeth all his bones: not one of them is broken"—a perfect description of Kenneth's "softest landing in the history of parachuting."

# Chapter Twenty-One

# Battle of Tinian Island

Centuries from now, military historians will still study the battle for Tinian Island as an example of a nearly perfect amphibious assault. Admiral Raymond Spruance, who commanded the Pacific fleet from late 1945 to early 1946, said, "The Tinian operation was probably the most brilliantly conceived and executed amphibious operation in World War II. And General Holland "Hownlin' Mad" Smith, a Marine commander who is considered the "father" of modern U.S. amphibious warfare, added, "Tinian was the perfect amphibious operation in the Pacific war."

Though it was located just 3.5 miles southwest of Saipan, the island of Tinian had a completely different geography that was much less formidable for attacking Marines. Measuring about 12.5 miles in length, and never more than five miles wide, the island was far less mountainous than Saipan. Its highest point, on the northern part of the island, was Mount Lasso at 564 feet, almost 1,000 feet lower than the highest point on Saipan. Another hill of almost the same height dominated the southern landscape. The topography of the rest of the island featured small rolling hills, many of them covered with sugar cane fields.

But if the interior of the island was less formidable for attacking forces, the same could not be said of the exterior. Like a plateau rising out of the sea, Tinian Island featured a coastline of rocky cliffs interrupted in only a few places with beaches. The best landing beaches were located on the southwest side of the island, near Tinian Town (now San Jose), but there were two other landing areas on the northwest corner of the island that each featured a small dent in the cliff line. These beaches, designated White Beach 1 and White Beach 2, were only 50 and 60 meters wide each, however. Landing an entire Marine division in such a small area could easily create a deadly bottleneck. But because the 9,000+ Japanese troops on the island did not expect a landing in such a narrow area, it was not heavily defended. A Marine reconnaissance mission, conducted under cover of darkness, revealed further information about White Beach 1 and White Beach 2. There were no man-made obstacles to obstruct a landing force, and the surrounding cliffs were only six to ten feet high, with small breaks that would enable troops to proceed inland, albeit single file, without the use of ropes, ladders or cargo nets.

Given this information, the Marine commanders formulated a brilliant attack strategy that caught the Japanese completely off guard, one of the few times during the war when U.S. forces achieved a complete tactical surprise.

For several days, battleships and aircraft shelled the area surrounding the beaches near Tinian Town. Then, on July 24, 1944, eight U.S. transports carrying two regiments from the 2nd Marine Division approached the beach and began lowering landing craft from the ships as the troops lowered themselves down the cargo net. The Japanese commanders on shore reacted immediately and committed their forces to Tinian Town.

But it was all a ruse.

The real landing was taking place on the White Beach 1 and White Beach 2, where the 4th Marine Division had crossed over from Saipan. The entire division landed unimpeded on the two tiny beaches before the Japanese caught on. Indeed, the Japanese forces at Tinian Town never left their defensive positions guarding the beach.

David Powell was glad there was little enemy opposition during the landing on White Beach 1 and 2. Otherwise, he would have been a sitting duck. The reefs at the landing site extended from the beach for several hundred yards. Because of the shallow water, no more than four feet at the deepest, the LSDs had to unload their tanks into the water as far as a quarter mile from the beach. Each tank had to be led in by a man on foot to keep the tank from grounding on the numerous shell holes and craters that had been knocked into the reef. As David led his tank in, he was thankful that there was only intermittent sniper fire.

By that night, the Marines were well dug in and prepared for a counterattack by the Japanese. Because of the rugged terrain, the tank platoons were stationed just behind the front lines. Mosquitoes were everywhere, and David and his platoon had to wear mosquito netting around their heads and place it over their foxholes to keep from being eaten alive. The calm soon ended when the Japanese launched the most furious counterattack that David was to experience during the entire war. The fighting lasted all night. The Japanese breached the American line, and at one point, David was receiving machine gun fire from both his front and rear. Eventually, the Japanese were driven back. Daylight revealed a landscape strewn with death and destruction. Everywhere David looked, there were bodies. In front of David's battalion alone, there were 1,300 Japanese dead.

On July 31, the Japanese made their last stand on the end of the island. As on Saipan, many Japanese chose suicide by jumping off cliffs rather than being caught by the Americans. Marine casualties were 328 dead and 1,571 wounded. Within four months, the 107th U. S. Naval Construction Battalion, Sea Bees, had built six airfields, each 2,400 meters in length, for use by the B-29 Superfortress. Soon Tinian was the busiest airfield of the war, with an installation housing 40,000 military personnel and a road system laid out like the island of Manhattan, with streets named accordingly. On July 26, 1945, the first operational atomic bomb, nicknamed

"Little Boy," was delivered by the U.S.S. Indianapolis to the island. Eleven days later, on August 6, the B-29 Enola Gay took off from Tinian Island, flew to a height of 30,700 feet over the city of Hiroshima and dropped the world's first atomic bomb.

David Powell

## Chapter Twenty-Two

# Swimming in Hurricanes

The 30 days of leave had passed quickly and in early August 1944, Delmar reported for duty at the U.S. Naval Hospital in Newport, Rhode Island. Because of his previous success and proven ability in the operating room, Delmar assumed that he would be assigned to once again assist a surgeon. But the naval bureaucracy was not so astute in its assessment. Instead of considering Delmar's talents, they assigned Delmar to the rather strange duty of managing the patients' stored gear. Apparently, the Navy thought that such a position would be less stressful and help Delmar recover from the shock of Omaha Beach. If a patient died, Delmar would inspect the soldier's personal belongings and remove any distasteful items, such as pornographic photos, that could serve as an embarrassment to family members. Delmar was stationed in the dark, dreary confines of a basement, and he found the work equally uninspiring.

Fortunately, the work didn't last long, and, as always, Delmar found ways to brighten up his life. In early September 1944, a major hurricane worked its way up the eastern seaboard of the United States. First spotted on September 9, northwest of the Lesser Antilles, the storm (which would probably be classified today as a Category 4 hurricane) and its 70-foot waves had already sunk the USS Warrington about 450 miles east of Vero Beach, Florida. As it neared the U.S coast, the storm took a more northerly course, sinking two Coast Guard cutters off the coast of North Carolina. Now with its eye just off shore, the hurricane ripped through eastern shore Maryland, then continued, like a circular saw, ripping up the coast line of Delaware and New Jersey, tearing up Atlantic City's boardwalk and smashing the city's famous Steel Pier. New York City was pummeled by 90-mph winds and the storm roared across Long Island and headed straight for Rhode Island and Delmar Powell.

The weather forecasters had predicted that the eye of the hurricane would pass over the Newport Naval Hospital, and when it did, Delmar and his fellow sailors were given orders to pick up all the window screens that had been blown out by the first half of the storm. So there was Delmar, standing in the calm air of the Great Atlantic Hurricane of 1944. As the men picked up the window screens, the nearby Atlantic Ocean was still wild and furious, teeming with whitecaps. Someone in the group joked about what a great time it would be to go for a swim. Delmar joked back, saying that he'd go in because he wasn't afraid of any old storm. Before he knew it, the joke became a bet. Five men each offered Delmar ten dollars if he would go for a swim in the angry ocean. It was the kind of "double dog dare" of a challenge that Delmar couldn't resist, especially with fifty dollars on the line! And besides, Delmar had a secret strategy. So the five bettors and the one "better" walked out to the end of a pier that jutted out some 50 feet from shore. Delmar stripped off his clothes and dove in. Instead of trying to swim on the surface, with its cacophony of wind and waves, Delmar dove down to the bottom of the sea and swam back to shore underwater. Down there, the sea was calm. On the pier, the bettors kept waiting for their swimmer to appear. When Delmar popped out of the sea at the shoreline, they looked at Delmar as if they were seeing a ghost. They thought that Delmar had drowned. Instead, they were met by wet and naked Delmar Powell, who was grinning from ear to ear as he promptly demanded his fifty well deserved bucks.

One of the many friends that Delmar made during his time in Newport was a sailor with the suggestive name of Dusty Rhodes. Dusty had been serving on an aircraft carrier when he fell headfirst down the large elevator shaft used to move aircraft back and forth from the flight deck and the holding bay below deck. The fall crushed his skull. Navy surgeons had replaced the skull fragments with a steel plate. After his rehabilitation was completed, Dusty was transferred to Newport where he and Delmar became close friends.

Just how close the two friends were became apparent when Dusty, driving his 1939 Studebaker, had an automobile accident in nearby Providence, Rhode Island. When the city police arrested Dusty, he was given the proverbial one phone call to make, but instead of calling the Shore Patrol or the hospital, as he should have, Dusty called Delmar, whom he knew was eating at a restaurant. Delmar took a cab to the Providence Police Station to bail out his friend. When he arrived, he could hear Dusty yelling and screaming behind a closed, locked door. Mean, gruff voices were shouting at Dusty, and then Delmar heard what sounded like the dull thwack of fist hitting bone. Delmar quickly walked down a hallway, lined with a long row of metal filing cabinets, to an office where three uniformed policemen were sitting at their desks. Delmar demanded that they stop the "interrogation" of Dusty in the other room immediately. The three policemen laughed and smirked. Delmar became infuriated. He smashed in the tops of two filing cabinets with his fists, then kicked two more over. Files and papers flooded the floor, and the three cops started to come after Delmar, who was ready for a fight and mad enough to think that he could handle all three. Suddenly, Delmar heard a loud voice behind him yell, "What's going on here?" It was a high ranking Naval officer, accompanied by two Shore Patrolman. Delmar told them about Dusty, and the officer and patrolmen said they had heard the same shouts from the locked room. The officer banged on the door to the room that held Dusty and identified himself. The door opened immediately to reveal a beaten and bruised Dusty Rhodes. The Naval officer, who was in charge of the Shore Patrol, was incensed. Whenever a soldier or a sailor got in trouble with the law, the local authorities were to notify the Shore Patrol immediately. He gave the police officers a real talking down, then took Dusty and Delmar outside and said, "You guys have had enough trouble tonight. If you can get your car running, I'll let you go back to the hospital and I won't even write up a report." Rusty and Delmar, who knew they better take advantage of the free ride out of trouble, immediately replied, "Yes sir," gave the officer a snappy salute and were gone.

Because they were AWOL, Delmar drove the car back to the base and hid the wrecked automobile in a wooded section near the hospital. By this time, dawn was breaking on the horizon as the two young sailors, fueled by adrenaline of youth, made their way to the cyclone fence in back of the hospital and started crawling under it. Their timing could not have been worse. Just as Delmar had made his way under the fence and was starting to help Dusty do the same, an automobile with two stars conspicuously displayed on the front bumper pulled up along side the curb. Of all the people who could have spotted them, it was no less than a rear admiral. A stern, authoritative voice yelled from the car, "What are you two men doing?"

Delmar Powell knew he was in a fix: Caught climbing under the fence of a United States Naval Base at dawn by nothing less than a two-star admiral, who could bring the whole weight and authority of his position to bear upon two nobodies like Dusty and Delmar. What could Delmar possibly say that would defuse the volatile situation and avoid charges of being AWOL all night? It was not an enviable position. Thinking quickly, as he always seemed to do in tight situations, Delmar came up with the perfect answer and shouted back, "I've got him, sir! I've got him." It was brilliant. The admiral immediately surmised that Delmar's buddy had tried to go AWOL and now Delmar was doing a heroic deed, trying to save his friend from a bad decision. "That's good sailor," yelled the admiral. "Just hold him right there, and I'll be right around." But Dusty and Delmar weren't about to stick around. They took off as fast as they could run, and by the time the admiral arrived at the scene of the crime, the two sailors were resting sweetly in their bunks inside the hospital. As Delmar lay there, all he could think was, "How in the world is this kind of duty helping the war effort?"

The question soon became irrelevant when Delmar received orders to report to Camp Bradford in Little Creek, Virginia, near the popular vacation spot, Virginia Beach. The Navy, it seemed, had come to its senses and was going to take full advantage of Delmar's skills by giving him training to work as the only medical man on an LST ship. The training was similar to the instruction Delmar had received to become a Pharmacist Mate: learning how to prepare solutions, tinctures, salves, ointments and other medicines. The training also involved physical conditioning, such as running an obstacle course, all in preparation for the amphibious landings that were routine at his next assignment. Delmar was headed to the Pacific.

But first, Delmar reported to duty at Jacksonville, Florida. His new ship was LST 357, now in dry dock and undergoing repair after seeing extensive action in North Africa and two amphibious landings in Italy. She had even been there with Delmar at Omaha Beach during the D-Day invasion. Many of her men had been killed or wounded in battle and Delmar was one of the replacements used to bring the crew to full strength for the work to be done in the Pacific Theater. Delmar felt an immense pride and satisfaction in serving on this battle-tested ship. The espirit de corps among the crew of LST 357 was high, and the ship even had a mascot. After completing a successful amphibious assault in Italy, some of the ship's officers went ashore. Among the ruins of a shelled out building, they found a large stuffed stork, which they immediately confiscated, thinking that such a fine specimen of a bird would make an admirable mascot for the ship,. The massive bird, with its spindly legs, white plumage and extended beak, stood proudly in the ship's wheelhouse, looking out to sea with a perennial gaze and a visage as mysterious as the Sphinx. The officers had even commissioned a talented enlisted artist on board to paint portraits of the stork on both sides of the officer's quarters and the wheelhouse. Why the officers had chosen a stork for the ship's mascot was revealed by the large letters printed above the imposing pictures: "WE DELIVER," the motto adopted by LST 357 many years before the U.S. Postal Service was to do the same. Just as the stork has a mission of delivering babies, so the crew of the LST delivered its cargo of men and equipment onto beaches across the world. Delmar felt proud to be part of a unit that kept its sense of humor even in the midst of tragedy and death.

On LST 357, Delmar served as a Pharmacist Mate on independent duty. In other words, Delmar was the ship's only medically trained specialist, responsible for providing medical treatment to a crew of 350 men plus any passengers or prisoners of war taken on board. If Delmar needed a medical doctor, he could request one by radio, but the Navy's physicians were stretched so thin that there was only one doctor on call for every 16 LSTs, also called a "Flotilla." This situation of providing medical care without the supervision of a medical doctor had become standard procedure during Delmar's service. Indeed, during the entire D-Day invasion, Delmar never once saw a doctor. There were two or three physicians on board, but they were too busy performing surgery to come to the tank deck where Delmar tended to the wounded. The Pacific Theater would be no different. Delmar never saw the one physician assigned to his flotilla.

In the dry docks of Jacksonville, the "We Deliver" was undergoing a complete transformation in preparation for a new kind of duty in a new section of the world. First equipped to fight in the European Theater, LST 357 had insulation against the cold of the North Sea and the English Channel installed in her bulkheads, and she had been painted a battleship gray to blend in with the foggy dreary weather so common in that sector of the world. Now that insulation was being ripped out, replaced by a different kind of material designed to keep out the tropical heat of the South Pacific. Fresh shades of green camouflage paint were applied to mask her appearance during island warfare. All this work was being done by civilian workers under contract from the Navy. As a result, the crew had nothing to do but wait. As the idle days slipped by, one after another, Delmar felt like he was on vacation. But soon the initial restfulness gave way to boredom. And nothing spells trouble more than a group of bored sailors.

The adventure began as Delmar and two of his shipmates were strolling along the shore of the St. Johns River, wiling away the hours, when they ran across a Landing Craft Vehicle Personnel (LCVP) tied up on shore. The LCVP is a small boat, designed to hold a platoon of men and one jeep, equipped with a bow ramp that dropped down to allow the men and machine to unload when it hit a beach. But the three sailors really weren't interested in making an amphibious landing. They wanted to take her for a ride.

So there they were, three sailors, foot loose and care free, on a leisurely cruise down the St. Johns River, no one to tell them what to do, no commanding officer to obey. The water was calm; they were happy and free.

On the other side of a low railroad bridge that spanned the river, the men caught sight of some fellow travelers who seemed as contented as they were: porpoises jumping and frolicking as they slowly made their way to the Atlantic. They wanted to join and chase the happy mammals, but the ramp on the boat was just a bit too high and unable to pass under the sturdy steel bridge. As the porpoises slowly moved downriver, Delmar's buddies resigned themselves to the situation. But for Delmar, this was an irresistible challenge. Quickly his mind concocted a possible solution. "Hey, I can get her under the bridge!" he yelled. His buddies weren't too sure. "Well then, prove it," they said. That was all the encouragement Delmar needed. He quickly took the helm of the boat and took her upstream about 50 yards, then turned her back around facing the bridge and gunned the motor. They were heading straight for the bridge at full throttle, the engine roaring and the two passengers giving each other bewildered looks. They were really moving, top speed, pushing out a large wake, with the bridge only a few yards away. Disaster seemed imminent. Then suddenly Delmar shut the engine down. The bow of the boat immediately dropped down just before the top hit the bridge and the boat's momentum carried it through to the other side, where, with perfect timing, the bow raised up to its normal position. Delmar had done it! The porpoises were just ahead. It was as if they had been waiting for them. So the three sailors spent the rest of the day cavorting with their newfound friends, exploring the river and leaving behind, if only temporarily, the scars and ravages of battles fought and battles to be won. Returning home, Delmar again successfully deployed his "sinking bow" trick, but when the three sailors pulled up to dock, their joy-filled day turned dark. Two Shore Patrolmen were waiting for them, and they escorted the three sailors to the Executive Officer. He gave them a stern warning and lecture about the misbehavior, but then quickly dismissed them without further punishment. Delmar even thought he detected a slight nearly hidden smile in the officer's face as he told the men to report back to their duty stations.

After many months of work, LST 357 was ready for duty. Delmar thought he had never seen a prettier ship, newly painted and rarin' to go. The ship's commander took her out into the Atlantic for a shake-down cruise, then took her into the docks at Davisville, Rhode Island. It was the summer of 1945, and the commander gave Delmar a week's leave for a very important reason. Delmar's brother Kenneth had been released from a German POW camp and had returned home to Hartford.

What a reunion it was! The two brothers who had shared a ride and worked together at the Pratt & Whitney plant had hardly communicated during the last three years as the war took them their separate ways. With their addresses changing so often, it had been almost impossible to write each other. Kenneth shared his POW experience, and the two quickly took up a pre-war hobby they had shared: playing tennis in Elizabeth Park in West Hartford. As Delmar was playing, he noticed a 1941 Buick pull up and park near the courts. A teenage girl got out of the car and walked over to the court where the two brothers were playing. "Hi fellas," she said, and the two brothers mumbled something in return, not knowing who the girl was. Suddenly, Delmar recognized her. It was Helen Pye. Delmar had met Helen in the summer of 1941 when she was a gawky 14-year-old. What a difference four years had made. Now Helen was 18 and every bit a woman, the pretty figure of a young lady. Delmar was smitten! That afternoon, after the tennis game, Delmar called her to see if she wanted to go to the movies that night.

Helen's answer almost ended the relationship before it began. "I knew you were going to call," she said during the phone conversation. The presumptuous tone of the remark angered Delmar, and he almost hung up on the girl. But love won out. The two double dated with Ken and a girl named Connie Deliver. After enjoying the movie and a soda, the foursome returned to Helen's home, and Ken accompanied Connie to her home, about a block away. When he returned, he took a seat on the street side curb to give his brother and Helen a bit of privacy as they said good night. He had to wait a good long while. As the young couple said their extended farewells, they were periodically interrupted by Helen's father. They could hear him clear his throat or "accidentally" drop a shoe on the floor or raise a window with a loud clatter—anything to remind his daughter and her new young sailor suitor of the lateness of the hour. By the time Delmar left, it was too late to catch the last bus, and he and Ken had to make the five-mile trek back home. But Delmar didn't care. He was in love.

He hardly slept that night. Too many things were happening. When the image of Helen wasn't filling his mind, Delmar thought about the coming morning. His ship was scheduled to leave at dawn, and Delmar was under strict orders not to tell anyone, including his family, that LST 357 was heading for the Pacific. At 3 a.m., he finished packing his belongings and returned to Davis Ville, Rhode Island. Long before Mom or Dad or Ken or Helen were awake, Delmar was headed out to sea. What the future held in terms of the war was unclear. But one thing was certain. If he did make it home, Delmar Powell was going to marry Helen Pye.

# Chapter Twenty-Three

# POW

★ ★ ★ ★

## Lt. Powell Missing In Raid on Germany

Two miles north of the village of Barth, on a strip of barren land jutting into the Baltic Sea, stood the German prison camp Stalag Luft 1. First built to house the prisoners captured during the English retreat at Dunkirk, it was the largest camp for air force prisoners in Nazi Germany, housing close to 5,000 inmates by the end of the war. A large pine forest bordered the camp's western edge, and to the east and north, the cold, fierce waters of Barth Harbor and the Baltic Sea were less than a mile away. Two rows of barbed wire, four feet apart and attached to 10-foot posts, encircled the camp, and every hundred meters, a guard tower, equipped with a

Lt. Kenneth R. Powell, a pilot, has been missing in action over Germany since July 16. This information has been received by his parents, Mr. and Mrs. H. D. Powell, 236 Laurel St.

Lieutenant Powell has been in the Army since October, 1942, when he joined a medical unit at Camp Pickett, Va. After transferring to the Army Air Forces, he was commissioned and trained at MacDill Field, Tampa, Fla., before his B-17 crew left for European service. Prior to enlistment he was employed at the Pratt & Whitney Aircraft plant.

He has two brothers in the service, Sgt. David D. Powell, serving with the Marines in the South Pacific and Delmar S. Powell, pharmacist's mate 2/c, who is now home on furlough after participating in the Normandy invasion. The youngest brother, Roger E. Powell, is awaiting call as an Army aviation cadet.

**Lt. Powell**

machine gun and a pair of spotlights, stood watch over the encampment. The Stalag was divided into five compounds, four prison compounds and a fifth area, in the center, where the prison's well constructed administrative buildings stood. The prisoners called this area "The Oasis" because its green grass and well trimmed shrubbery stood in such contrast to the surrounding muddy ground and shabby prison huts.

When Kenneth Powell arrived at Stalag 1 in early August 1944, the Germans were still constructing the prison barracks for North 2 Compound. Until construction was finished, the newly arriving prisoners were assigned to a tent village. Once, when the new prisoners heard and then saw planes of the Eighth Air Force fly overhead, they spilled out of their tents by the hundreds and sent up a loud cheer to their fellow airmen overhead. The Germans were so enraged by this demonstration that they threatened to shoot and kill any prisoner who did not remain in his tent during an air raid. That put a damper on any external exhibitions, but whenever the Eighth Air Force flew overhead, each man was cheering silently in his heart.

Within three or four weeks, Kenneth and the other prisoners were assigned to the newly constructed barracks in North 2 Compound. Each room housed 20 men, with the beds stacked three high around the outside wall. In the center, there was just enough space for a table and room to walk around it. North 2 Compound was an officer's camp, and the Germans gave special privileges to officers. The enlisted men housed in other compounds of the camp were assigned to work duty in factories and on farms. In contrast, the officers of Stalag 1 at Barth had a life of leisure.

Packages from the American Red Cross, the YMCA and other sources supplied the officers with sporting equipment and library books. Softball games were a common occurrence. Some of the men kept in shape doing chin-ups on exercise bars. There was always a card game going, and the more artistic officers even put on theatrical productions, with some of the men dressed as women to play the female roles. There was even a small orchestra that played concerts. Kenneth read three books during his time as a POW, but for the most part, he spent his time tinkering with tin.

A geared egg beater was Kenneth's first creation. The food parcels from the Red Cross contained powdered milk in a tin can labeled KLIM (milk spelled backwards). But when the men mixed the KLIM powdered milk with water, it would always lump up. Beating it with a fork didn't help much, either. That's when Kenneth got the idea to make an egg beater using a KLIM can, barbed wire and a bed slat. First, Kenneth traded cigarettes (he didn't smoke) with a German guard for little pieces of aluminum wire to be used as brads. Kenneth then used a file to cut saw teeth on the back edge of a table knife. Using this handmade saw, he carved a bed slat into a handle for the egg beater. (Ken and the other men were always taking out the wooden bed slats that supported their mattresses and

A geared egg beater was Kenneth's first creation. It was quite an engineering feat with the materials available.

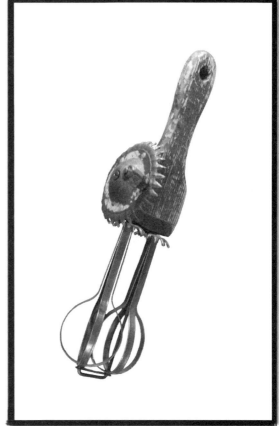

transforming them into useful tools. By the time of their liberation, their sawdust-filled mattresses were so unsupported, they had to place flattened pieces of cardboard from the Red Cross parcels under the mattress to prop them up.) He also used the knife to cut the top and bottom off a KLIM can and then cut these into thin strips. Using the end of a shoe brush as a hammer, Kenneth shaped the strips of tin into the gears and other working parts of the egg beater. He was a regular tinsmith. The last thing he needed was a screw to use as an axle for the gears. Another cigarette trade took care of that, and then all the pieces were secured using the aluminum tin brads.

Unfortunately, the first prototype didn't work. The single strips of tin were too thin and not strong enough. Kenneth went back to work, folding the tin strips twice to quadruple their width and strength. This time, the egg beater worked beautifully. It was sturdy, too. All 20 men in his room used the egg beater every day to mix the KLIM milk. Kenneth still has the egg beater, and it still works.

Kenneth was always looking for new projects that required the use of his mechanical skills. He made pans and dishes out of tin that were used for eating and

Blower forced air over the coke to make the oven hot.

cooking. But his most sophisticated achievement was building a clock. For almost seven months, Kenneth, Al Thomas and Winthrop (Win) Worcester worked on the project. Thomas was a graduate engineer from Alabama, and Worcester was a naturally talented craftsman. Powell's experience at Pratt Whitney in design and drawing gears for airplane engines also proved helpful. Worcester worked on the frame that housed the clock. Thomas designed the gear mechanism, and Powell used his tinsmith skills, plus a knife and the butt of a shoe brush, to cut and shape the gears. After Powell finished the first gear, Thomas determined it did not have the right number of teeth, and Powell started working on a second version. He ended up making several gears of various sizes to meet Thomas's strict specifications as well as a ratchet to control the timing of the pendulum. The clock was powered by gravity. A fairly heavy rock, secured near the ceiling of the room, was attached to the ratchet of the clock. The weight of the rock set the moving parts in motion, and by setting the pendulum weight at the right setting, the clock kept time with amazing precision. It took about two days for the rock to make its way from the ceiling to the floor. Winding the clock was simply a matter of lifting the rock back to the ceiling and starting the process all over again.

Oven as it was set up in the barrack.

Twenty-five years after the war, Al Thomas presented the first unused gear that Kenneth had made and placed it on his desk. "I've had it for 25 years," said Al. "Now it's your turn." Many of the artifacts created by the prisoners were saved and made their way to a POW exhibit at Wright Patterson Air Force Base in Dayton, Ohio.

Cooking was a passion in the barracks. In Kenneth's barracks, the men

123

Oven built by Kenneth in the camp, now on display at W.P.AFB museum in Dayton, Ohio.

took turns as cooks, two new men each week. The men kept what they wanted from the weekly Red Cross parcels and then turned over the rest to the cooks. Trying to concoct something good to eat from the foodstuffs in the parcels became almost an obsession among the prisoners.

By mixing crumbled-up graham crackers with KLIM powdered milk and pitted prunes, the prisoners made a kind of cake batter they cooked in an oven that Kenneth had made with the tin from the KLIM cans. The oven was designed to be part of the chimney on the stove. It was made with double sides, bottom and top, with a 2-inch space in between so the smoke from the stove would come up the chimney into that space at the bottom, then around and up the sides, and over the top of the oven, and then go on out the upper part of the chimney above the oven.

The door of the oven was made with two walls of tin filled with sand to hold the heat in. It was hard to keep the coke burning in the stove hot enough to heat the room in the winter, so Kenneth built a blower from tin and wood from the bed slats to keep the coke burning hot.

The prisoners even managed to make "prison fudge," mixing powdered milk, chocolate from the D Bars, sugar and then adding chopped-up prune pits which, roasted in the oven, tasted like almonds. Some of the men even managed to distill prunes and raisins and create a wine-like moonshine they called "Four Raisins" after a popular wine of the time, "Four Roses"

Nobody liked the margarine that came in the Red Cross parcels. It tasted like lard. The margarine supplied by the Germans tasted far better although it certainly wasn't up to gourmet standards. Indeed, the German margarine, together with some jelly, was the only way to make the hard, dark German barley bread edible. The prisoners put the American margarine to a more innovative function. They cut a slit in the margarine can, then cut a piece of an Army belt and inserted it into the slit. After soaking up the margarine oil, the belt became a wick and the soldiers had a lamp.

At night, the men talked about their families and their lives back home. One night, the barracks had to turn a bench into a cot to make room for a new prisoner who had just been captured. He talked about his being shot down, and when he had finished, there was a long silence. Then suddenly, all at once, 20 voices yelled, "Hard luck!" It was their way of saying to the prisoner, "You're one of us."

The next day, Kenneth was washing his hands at an outdoor wash basin. The new prisoner was talking to another POW, and they discovered they were from the same town. They each pulled out their wallet to

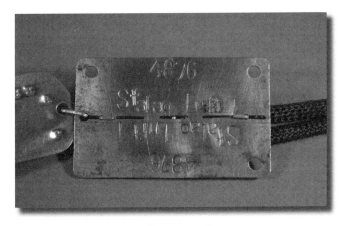

Kenneth's prison ID tag

show pictures of their wives. The new prisoner showed his picture first, and when he did, the other POW, who had been shot down more than a year before, yelled, "Hey, that's my wife!" He showed the picture in his wallet, and it was the same girl.

The Germans had a bulletin board set up in Compound II where they posted "up to date" information about the progress of the war. But the board was always at least two weeks behind what the prisoners already knew by listening to the radio broadcast of the BBC. British POWs who had been captured at Dunkirk had smuggled in the parts of a radio, which was assembled every day to get the BBC news, then taken apart and each piece hidden separately. The news was written on pieces of paper called a "POW WOW," and copies were smuggled into each barrack, quickly read, and then immediately burned.

Thanks to the radio, the prisoners knew about the rapid advance Patton was making with the Third Army. Two POWs made a bet that was announced to everyone in Compound II. One prisoner said they would be home for Christmas. The other POW said they wouldn't. As the more optimistic POW put it, "If we're not home by Christmas, I'll kiss your ass in front of the whole compound." The bet was on.

Soon after that, the news arrived over the BBC that the Germans had broken through the Allied lines at Bastogne as part of The Battle of the Bulge. During that brutally cold winter, some of the American soldiers captured at Bastogne were brought to Stalag 1. They were amputees, victims of frostbite from having fought so long in their fox holes.

The morning after hearing the bad news about Bastogne was Christmas Day.

There was a foot of snow on the ground, and the men were standing in formation for the daily roll call. After they had accounted for everybody, the Germans, as they almost always did, dismissed the troops. But this time, the prisoners just stayed in place—except for two men. They walked quickly into a barracks and soon returned. One of them had a towel draped over his shoulder, a wash rag and soap in one hand and a bucket of steaming water in the other hand. The other man turned around with his back to the formation, stooped over and pulled his pants down, showing

This star was made by Ken Powell from the tin of a KLIM can to go on the Christmas tree, 1944, Stalag 1, Barth, Germany. When liberated by the Russians May 1, 1945, Pilot Willie Johnson took the star with him, and it has been on top of his family Christmas tree every year since the war.

his butt in that cold air. The man with the bucket of hot water took the wash rag and soap, lathered it up good, washed off the bare butt, and then bent down and kissed the lily-white bottom.

The bet had been paid—in full.

Unfortunately, as was often the case in the P.O.W. camp, this light-hearted mood soon gave way to a more somber tone. A Colonel Spicer, angered by the news about Bastogne and German officers' unprofessional and sometimes abusive treatment of the camp's POW officers, addressed the troops, warning them not to get "buddy/buddy" with the guards. The Germans considered Spicer a real troublemaker, and his speech was so severe in its criticism that they sentenced him to be executed and placed him in solitary confinement.

The Red Cross parcels that came for Christmas contained special foods. Kenneth's barracks received a turkey, which they baked, complete with dressing, in Kenneth's oven. Cookies sent by family members were shared and one fellow prisoner even made a desert that tasted like butterscotch. Kenneth made a Christmas tree from tin and the gold foil found on the jars of margarine. They decorated the tree with ornaments and crowned it with a little three-dimensional tin silver star. Willie took that little star with him when the camp was liberated, and it has hung on the Johnson Christmas tree every year.

There were four Army chaplains in Stalag 1 These four men had actually volunteered to become prisoners in order to minister to the spiritual needs of the men. One was a Catholic priest, and the other three were Protestants from England. On Christmas Day, the four chaplains received permission to have prisoners from all the compounds to gather together for a Christmas service. Each chaplain conducted a part of the service.

Letters from home helped brighten the long days. The letters were written on Form 111, a piece of paper measuring 10-3/4 x 5-1/2 inches and folded like a letter, with the address and return address on two of the panels. The other panels contained ruled lines for the letter, which had to be typed or written in block letters. Kenneth's parents wrote the following on February 28, 1945:

MY OWN DEAR DARLING SON, KENNETH,

THIS IS A BEAUTIFUL, BRIGHT SUNNY DAY WITH THE FEELING OF SPRING IN THE AIR AND THE SNOW IS RAPIDLY MEILTING AWAY. SOON THE BUDS WILL BEGIN TO SWELL AND THE BIRDS TO SING, AND I PRAY IT WILL BRING YOU HOME ONCE MORE.

HOW IS EVERYTHING GOING THERE IN CAMP? WHAT BOOKS HAVE YOU BEEN READING LATELY? HAVE YOU BEEN PLAYING ANY BASEBALL? DID YOU DO ANY SWIMMING IN THE BALTIC SEA LAST SUMMER OR WAS IT TOO COLD THEN?

WE ARE ALL FINE HERE AT HOME. DADDY WORKING HARD AS EVER AT THE SAME WORK, QUITE LONG HOURS, TOO.

HARRY JR. WORKED IN A GREENHOUSE DURING THE WINTER VACATION. THEY ARE ALL BACK IN SCHOOL NOW, AND EVERYTHING IS SAILING RIGHT ALONG.

WE HAVE HAD A GOOD LETTER FROM ROGER, AND HE IS PLANNING TO RUN COMPETITION WITH YOU SOME DAY. HE IS FINE. SAYS HE MET A CUTE LITTLE GIRL IN ONE OF THE CHURCHES.

A GOOD LETTER FROM DEL SAYS HE IS SURE A BUSY FELLOW. HE WAS GOING OVER TO SEE JOHN SILLIMAN LAST SUNDAY FOR THEY ARE NOT VERY FAR APART.

SENT A LETTER TO CLARIECE, BUT IT CAME BACK SO I DON'T KNOW WHERE THEY ARE. BUDDY IS THROUGH-SENT US A SWELL PICTURE OF HIM.

WE HAVE HAD NO WORD FROM DAVID FOR A LONG TIME NOW, BUT THINK WE KNOW WHERE HE IS.

WELL DEAR, HURRY HOME. WE LOVE YOU AND ARE PRAYING TO SEE YOU SOON,

LOVE AND PRAYERS-MOTHER AND DADDY

About 30 days after coming home, not long after VJ Day,
at Atlantic City, N.J., Ritz Carlton.

While there, Kenneth made the decision to stay in the Air Force to fly.

# Chapter Twenty-Four

# Rumors of War

After going to Hell and back, David Powell was now in Paradise. Having survived the bloody campaigns on Saipan and Tinian, David and his crew had been shipped back to the island of Maui. Here, for just a few days, they enjoyed a few days of R&R. But soon, the unit was back together, retraining, receiving new replacements and preparing for the next operation.

They boarded a ship and set off to sea. No one knew where they were going. For several days, rumors and speculation were rampant. Then, the officers broke out the maps and showed them a tiny speck of land in the Pacific Ocean that was their destination.

The place was called Iwo Jima.

About eight square miles in size, 1/3 the area of the island of Manhattan, Iwo Jima is a volcanic island almost equidistant between Tokyo and Saipan. Fighting aircraft based on the island's two airfields often attacked the B-29s now bombing the Japanese homeland, and a radar installation on the island warned the homeland of the impending bombing attacks. Now more than 110,000 Marines and 880 ships were congregating around this little piece of real estate. When they arrived, it constituted the largest Armada invasion up to that time in the Pacific Theater.

It took David's convoy more than a month to arrive on the scene. David and his men were aboard a Landing Ship, Medium (LSM), which could hold five tanks. Small and slow, the ship rolled and rocked in the open sea for 40 days and 40 nights until they arrived at Iwo Jima. For the next 35 days, they would return to Hell.

## Marines Take Cover After Landing on Iwo Beach

Fourth Division Marines take cover in abandoned Jap trench and craters made by bombing after they hit beach in invasion of Iwo Jima. Note battered Jap ship (right background).
—[AP Wirephoto

# Chapter Twenty-Five

# Battle of Iwo Jima

Perhaps no other battle in history better demonstrates the fighting spirit of the United States Marines than Iwo Jima.

The battle began shortly before 2 a.m. on February 19, 1945, with a naval bombardment that seemed to leave the entire island on fire. Soon more than 110 American bombers filled the sky and pounded the tiny island with the longest sustained aerial offensive of the war. According to Admiral Chester Nimitz, "No other island received as much preliminary pounding as did Iwo Jima." Yet the effect was minimal. The underground fortresses and 18 miles of tunnels built by the 22,000 Japanese soldiers deep into the island's volcanic rock were hardly touched.

There were two landing beaches, on the southeast and western shores. Between these two landing areas, at the southern tip of the island, stood Mount Suribachi, its 550-foot height dominating the landscape.

The Japanese were ready. From the heights of Mount Suribachi, Japanese gunners could zero in on every square inch of the two landing beaches. In fact, every Marine on the island was within range of Japanese fire. Blockhouses and pillboxes flanked the landing areas, ready to lay down a deadly interlocking crossfire. Rockets, anti-boat and anti-tank guns were also trained on the beaches. The Japanese commander, Lieutenant General Tadamichi Kuribayashi knew that, lacking any kind of naval or air support, his men were doomed and the fall of the island was inevitable. Still he was determined to make the Americans pay dearly for their invasion. He knew that the American forces would be unable to dig foxholes and take cover in the volcanic ash of the beaches. He ordered that his forces not fire upon the initial landing forces until the Marines reached a line of machine gun nests and the beaches were filled with enemy soldiers. Later, during the last desperate days of the battle, Kuribayashi ordered his troops not to conduct a bonsai charge, which he considered ineffective because the screams of the soldiers gave the enemy advance notice. Instead, he ordered a "silent" charge.

THE HARTFORD TIMES, FRIDAY, FEBRUARY 23, 1945

## 'Impregnable' Japanese Pillbox Seized by Marines on Iwo

American Marines, invading Jap stronghold of Iwo Jima, dig in after taking what enemy considered was "impregnable" pillbox (center background). Note Marine in center, digging foxhole, and bodies, some in open, some partly covered by sand, which the caption did not identify.—[AP Wirephoto

At 08:59, the first wave of Marines hit the beaches.

David's tank platoon was assigned to the right flank of the 4th Marine Division, which landed on the southeast beach. Their mission was to support the infantry troops as they drove straight inland and captured an airfield about 600 yards from the beach, then turn right and capture a large rock quarry that the Japanese had used for mining sulfur. All this was to be accomplished on the first day theoretically. The entire beach area was heavily mined, and by the time David's platoon came ashore on the third wave, the area was littered with the burning carcasses of blown-up tanks and amphibious tractors. David's tank, the first off the landing craft, made it safely to shore, thanks to a young engineer who guided them through the mine field. After going a few hundred yards inland, the tanks turned right toward the quarry and followed the tanks of the platoon commander, Lt. Tom Clifford, and the platoon sergeant, Joe Bruce. Almost immediately, the lieutenant's tank was hit, injuring Clifford and two or three other men. As the men were being evacuated, another barrage of Japanese fire destroyed Bruce's tank, leaving only David's tank and two others to carry on with the mission.

David continued the attack. He knew the area to the right of the tanks was mined. The area to the left was unknown territory, but it was their only option. Before advancing, the three tanks opened up with a massive barrage of machine gun fire and artillery shells to destroy any anti-tank guns that were located on their left side, closest to the airfield. Then David directed the driver to move forward. Fortunately, the area had no mines, or at least they didn't hit any. The three tanks, now about halfway between the airfield and the rock quarry, about 500 yards from the beach, advanced eastward with a cliff on their left. Occasionally, friendly fire from a nearby destroyer rocked the cliff face, the ship's gunnery sergeant trying to provide cover for the advancing tanks. Out of nowhere, an explosion rocked David's tank, followed by three of four more explosions. David couldn't tell whether it was a 3-inch gun or a 75mm gun, but whatever it was, the fire was going to knock out his tank if they didn't get it first. He and his gunner looked desperately for the origin of the fire. Suddenly, up in the cliff face, David saw a bright flash in a cave. He immediately called to his gunner and pointed to the location of the enemy fire. The gunner quickly took aim and fired. But he wasn't the only one. The gunnery officer on the destroyer had also spotted the Japanese position. Just as David's round exploded, the destroyer fired a broadside that literally lifted the whole side of the cliff and sent it tumbling down. The tanks received no more fire from that cliff side. But now David was stuck: the track on the right side of the tank had been blown off. It was the only time during the entire war that David's tank was immobilized.

At this point in the fight, with David's tank platoon far out in front of the infantry, he and his crew waited for the infantry to catch up. For the rest of the fight on Iwo Jima, the tank platoon was stationed near this site to guard an assembly area. Around them, for 34 more days, the fighting raged. Finally, the island was declared officially secured on March 26. Only 216 Japanese soldiers were captured alive, the rest of the more than 22,000 on the island were killed or, in some cases, committed suicide. Among Allied soldiers, almost 7,000 were killed, with more than 20,000 missing or injured.

Perhaps Admiral Chester W. Nimitz said it best, "Among the men who fought on Iwo Jima, uncommon valor was a common virtue."

# Iwo Resistance Fanatical

Aboard Admiral Turner's Expeditionary Force Flagship Off Iwo —(AP) — Marine Lt.-Gen. Holland Smith saw clear indications today that "our fanatical enemy will fight to the bitter end" on Iwo Jima.

"It must not be forgotten," said the rugged, hard-hitting general, "that the Japs consider Iwo part of their homeland.

"They have caused us some very serious difficulties. There has been a large amount of wreckage of boats, LVTS and ducks. But there have been sufficient rations, water and ammunition."

S/Sgt. David Dempsey, New York Marine combat corespondent, described a section of the beach where troops landed four days ago as "a scene of indescribable wreckage. And the wreckage is ours.

"You can see amphibian trac-tors turned upside down like pancakes on a griddle, derricks brought ashore to unload cargo tilted at insane angles where shells blasted them; anti-tank guns smashed before they had a chance to fire a shot.

"Even bulldozers had heavy casualties. Artillery could not be landed for 24 hours.

"Death . . . has taken possession of our beach. The officer in charge of a tank landing boat has been blown in half, trying to free his boat from the sand.

"Marines killed on the beach were buried by the tide."

# Whole Blood, Flown to Iwo, Saves Lives of Many Yanks

Iwo, Volcano Islands—(AP)— Large scale administration of whole blood forwarded from the United States has saved an uncounted number of lives in the goriest battle of the Pacific war, according to Comdr. R. S. Silvis, Fourth Marine Division, surgeon.

The blood was flown in iced containers from San Francisco to Guam and brought daily by plane to this battlefront where the Yanks and the Japanese are savagely contesting for a tiny bit of lava on the ocean highway to Tokyo.

There is no shortage yet, Silvis said, but "tell the folks at home to keep it coming."

Silvis said plasma is nearly as efficient as whole blood in shock cases, but not for injuries with heavy hemorrhages.

137

## Chapter Twenty-Five

# The Beginning of the End

There were hundreds of 18-year-old Army Air Corps cadets at the base in Biloxi, Mississippi, and they were all highly motivated, including Roger Powell. If he failed, if he "washed out" as a pilot, Roger would be reassigned a less glamorous military specialty such as being a gunner. So he applied himself with great intensity to the daily battery of mental and physical tests, from geometry class to the obstacle course.

From Biloxi, it was on to Laughlin Air Force Base near Del Rio, Texas. Laughlin was a flying school for training pilots of the B-26 "Marauder." This twin-engine medium bomber was nicknamed the "Widowmaker" because of its high rate of crashes during take-off. Here Roger served as a flight engineer before being sent to a base near Dodge City, Kansas, where he continued these duties: warming up the engines in the morning before flight and then accompanying the pilots as they practiced different maneuvers and touch-and-go landings. It was a long eight-hour day.

It was at Dodge City that Roger heard the news that the Japanese had surrendered. The war was over. The Army gave him two choices: complete the pilot training or reccive an honorable discharge. Having not even graduated from high school, Roger chose to be discharged and complete his schooling. In some respects, Roger felt disappointed, felt like he had stayed on the sidelines during the biggest game of the season, of any season. But then again, he had served his country. And then again, he was still alive.

# Chapter 26

# Liberation

By late April 1945, the German prison guards at Stalag 1 knew that the war was lost. The young German guards were now gone, called up to the front lines, replaced by much older soldiers who wore World War I uniforms with leggings wrapped below their knees. Once Kenneth looked skyward and saw a large squadron of Allied planes flying overhead, and then heard a nearby German captain mutter, "All ist kaput." Kenneth knew the end of his captivity was nearing.

Around midnight on May 1, 1945, the German prison guards at Stalag 1 climbed down from the towers and silently disappeared. Knowing that the Russians were just hours away, they slinked away into the anonymity of the night, hoping to return, undetected, to civilian life. When the prisoners realized that the Germans had abandoned the camp, a joyous pandemonium ensued. They busted out of the barracks, broke down fences and burned the hated watch towers. That morning, the Russians arrived and announced the camp liberated. For Kenneth, the feeling of liberation was indescribable, akin to the realization he had as a 10-year-old that Christ had set him free.

*If the Son therefore shall make you free, you shall be free indeed.*
John 8:36


A feast was in order. Instead of the standard, boring fare of rutabaga and barley bread supplied by the Germans and occasionally supplanted by Red Cross parcels, the prisoners were going to fill their bellies on an American delicacy: barbeque. The Russians rounded up a herd of cows and brought them into camp. With 5,000 men in camp, there were plenty of former butchers and meat cutters ready to go to work. Every barbeque needs a pit to cook the meat on, so the other soldiers commenced to digging a trench more than one block long. Firewood collected from the now abandoned buildings as well as the surrounding forests was thrown into the ditch and set ablaze. When the fire had burned down to red-hot coals, the men threw in barbed wire to serve as the grill and then on went the slabs of meat. There was even barbeque sauce to sop the meat in. Some innovative Yanks had created the flavorful sauce using a mixture of ingredients from the Red Cross parcels. North 2 Compound had a barbeque the likes of which the world had never seen, and probably never will again.

The Allied commander of the camp, Colonel Zemke, had been given an order that the prisoners remain in the camp until B-17s arrived to fly them out. But with the walls of the prison now destroyed, many of the men could not resist the sweet taste of freedom. They had had enough of this place called Stalag 1. About 2,000 prisoners took off on their own, traveling west to the American lines and hooking up with a unit. Laverro and Malloy took off, but Johnson and Powell decided to wait for the arrival of the planes.

The two toured the countryside as they waited for the planes. It was often a grisly sight. On the way to the town of Barth, they saw three older German women and two children lying dead in the water, shot in the head, most likely by Russian soldiers crazed with a desire for revenge. The town of Barth had been stripped bare.

At a nearby German air field, Kenneth found a flare gun (which he still has today) and two bags of flares, which he set off at night in a Fourth of July celebration.

The flare gun came in handy a few days later. Attached to each barracks was a small room containing a portable latrine. Every morning, a work detail carried the latrine outside, emptied the contents and let it air out. Use of the latrine by anybody other than barrack members was strictly forbidden; so when an interloper was spotted using the facility, Kenneth took out his flare gun and shot a red flare right over his head. It was very effective.

Kenneth had arrived at Stalag 1 by jumping out of a badly damaged B-17. It was only appropriate that he should leave the prison in a Flying Fortress. The newly liberated men flew to a small airfield in France and then were taken by train to Camp Lucky Strike. During the trip, the train, full of exuberant newly liberated Allies soldiers, stopped at a little French railroad station. Soon another train came along and stopped on some tracks just a few feet away. Every railroad car on this train contained hundreds of barrels with big round spouts on the side, about five inches in diameter. The train was hauling thousands of gallons of wine! When the young men, already intoxicated by their newfound freedom, realized the contents of the cargo, they couldn't contain themselves. They rushed out of the train, picked up any kind of container that could hold the wine, broke the spouts open and began to drink France's finest as if they were Bacchus himself. The wine flowed and flowed, and the men drank and drank. Moderation was unthinkable. Finally, some French authorities came upon the drinking orgy and ordered the men back on the train. The French were irate, and though they did not know it, their alcohol would soon enact its own revenge. The imbibers of the wine soon became sick on the train and began throwing up. The smell was so putrid that Kenneth got out of the railroad car at the next stop and rode on top of the train until they reached Camp Lucky Strike.

A huge installation of more than 1,500 acres, Camp Lucky Strike was the principal station for liberated POWs. It was located in Normandy, near the city of

Le Havre, and at the time of Kenneth's arrival, housed 40,000 liberated prisoners. Life at Camp Lucky Strike was boring. There was nothing to do but wait—no duties, no responsibilities—just sitting around the tent until the right boat landed to take you back to America. Many of the men that Kenneth met there had been waiting up to four weeks. Finally, Kenneth couldn't take it any more. He was going stir crazy with nothing to do. So he walked out to a road, stuck out his thumb and hitchhiked his way to the city of Paris. He was now officially AWOL, but nobody seemed to care. In fact, there were so many former American prisoners AWOL in Paris that the Army had set up a special PX there even though there was no official American military base in the City of Lights. Kenneth stayed with a French family that included two teenage girls and their 10-year-old brother. The soles of the little boy's shoes were completely gone, a vivid sign to Kenneth of the hardships the French people had endured under the Nazi regime since 1940. When Kenneth went to the PX and bought the boy a pair of shoes, he was stunned by the immensity of their gratitude. The two teenage girls didn't speak English, and Kenneth didn't speak French, but none of that seemed to matter. It was time, Kenneth thought, to have some fun, with not one but two girls on his arm. They used sign language to communicate as they made their way through Paris. They rode *La Grande RouÈ*, the giant Parisian Ferris wheel, three to a seat, walked down the Champs D'Elysees and the Arc De Triomphe, visited the Notre Dame Cathedral and Napoleon's tomb, and tried to see the art treasures of The Louvre, which unfortunately was closed. What at time it was! He was a free man in Paris. But all good things must pass. When Kenneth returned to Camp Lucky Strike, no notice was taken of his being AWOL for a week. The war was over. The rules had been relaxed, and soon Kenneth was on a ship bound for America.

Crossing the Atlantic was an ordeal. Kenneth's body was covered with red itchy spots the size of the end of a finger. Apparently, in Paris he had slept on a mattress filled with bed bugs. He took salt water showers to relieve the itching, and by the time the ship docked in New York, the spots were gone.

From New York the liberated POW took a ferry across the Hudson River to New Jersey where a train was waiting to take him to Fort Devens, Massachusetts. As he waited, Kenneth and another liberated POW walked up the track and met the engineer of the coal-burning steam engine, who asked them if they wanted to ride in the cab with him. "Sure! Thanks!" they said and climbed aboard. That steam engine got up to about 50 or 60 miles an hour going around the curves that followed the shore of the Hudson River all the way up to Albany, New York. Although the engine rocked from side to side as if it were about to leap the tracks, the scenes along the Hudson were thrillingly beautiful. For Kenneth, it was a real "Welcome home!" experience.

From Albany Kenneth took a bus to Fort Devens, then another train to Hartford. Before him stood the house on Highland Avenue. His family was not expecting him. Kenneth walked in the front door unannounced. The greeting was pure joy. He was home.

# Chapter Twenty-Seven

# Semper Fi

The bloody battle of Iwo Jima had taken its toll on the 4th Marine Division. Rumors flew that the division was to report to Saipan and then stand in reserve for the invasion of Okinawa. But fortunately, it was not to be. The division had suffered so many casualties that it was sent back to Maui, where the people had petitioned Congress to bring the 4th Marine Division back to their island. So the 4th Marine Division boarded ship and headed back to their adopted homeland.

On the second day at sea, David Powell received a major surprise, one that would change the course of his life. After enlisting as a buck private in 1941, Powell had advanced steadily up the ranks. By the time he arrived at the island of Roi, he was a buck sergeant, driving the lieutenant's tank and commanding the vehicle when the lieutenant was absent. On Saipan, the lieutenant worked almost exclusively at the infantry battalion command post as a liaison officer, passing on information to David, who now was effectively serving as the platoon commander. And on Iwo Jima, when the lieutenant was injured during the first phase of the operation, Powell again became the platoon's commanding officer.

This leadership experience had not gone unnoticed. With the 4th Marine Division sailing back to Maui from Iwo Jima, Powell was called in to meet the Company Commander, who asked if he wanted to accept a commission as a Second Lieutenant. Powell was totally surprised and didn't know what to say. Finally he asked the Commander, "Why?"

The Commander explained that he wanted to recommend Powell for the commission because of the leadership qualities he had exhibited under fire, but he didn't want to make the recommendation unless Powell would accept it.

For David, it was the greatest honor he could think of receiving. He told the officer that he would accept the commission. Sometime during their retraining in Maui, David Powell received his commission as a second lieutenant in the United States Marine Corps. By now, the unit had received replacements and was in full training. Word had it that the 4th Marine Division was preparing to recapture Wake Island, a small atoll in the North Pacific that had been bypassed by American forces, as a preparation for the invasion of Japan. But David and his men never found out if the rumors were true. With the atomic bombings of Hiroshima and Nagasaki, the Japanese surrendered on August 15, 1945.

The war was over. David was going home.

When he got back to the States, David was ordered to report to the Brooklyn Navy Yard, where he received a 10-day leave. David rushed up to Hartford to see his family: Mom, Dad, his wife Martie and his two sons, whom he had not seen in almost two years. When he had left in January 1944, Harry was three years old and David Jr. was just an infant. Now they were five and two, and their change in appearance and development was stunning. After three amphibious landings on enemy beaches, after scores of sleepless nights waiting for the Japanese to counterattack, after seeing countless men, including many friends, killed and injured, for the next 10 days, David was truly in paradise; he was with his family.

Unfortunately, any earthly paradise must come to an end. David soon received orders releasing him from active duty with the option of either staying in the Marine

Corps Reserve as a platoon sergeant or receiving a complete discharge. David chose the former, convinced that the United States and Russia would soon be at war and wanting to contribute his part as a Marine when it happened. He and Martie settled down in Anderson, Indiana, where David went back to work in the retail grocery business. In 1948, he was promoted to First Lieutenant in the Marine Corps Reserve, and in 1950 was called back to active duty for the Korean War. After that, David made a career with the Marine Corps, retiring in 1969 with the rank of Lieutenant Colonel.

In 1994, David was diagnosed with cancer. A few months before his death, he received a letter from a friend named "Shook," a gunner in his tank platoon. The letter concludes:

What you are going though now is what we all fear will happen to us.
I know that you are a believer, and if there is a heaven, I'm sure you will be there—and most of the "A" Company eventually.

To quote a poem once written, titled, "A Marine." (I only remember the last few lines)

And when he gets to Heaven,
To St. Peter he will tell,
"Another Marine reporting sir,
I've served my time in Hell."

I think in that respect, I'll probably make it there myself—If I don't get a chance to see you before—I'll see you there.

Semper Fi

# Chapter Twenty-Eight

# The Island of My Dreams

Southward she sailed down the Atlantic coast of America, stopping a the Navy Yard at Norfolk, then sailing past Jacksonville off the starboard beam. The next morning, LST 357 arrived at the U.S. Naval Base in Guantanamo Bay, Cuba, taking on fuel and supplies. A day later, before first light, the call "Anchors aweigh," announced the start of the ship's continuing voyage, southwest through the Caribbean Sea and then through the Panama Canal. Delmar was amazed by this engineering wonder. When the canal opened to world commerce on August 15, 1914, ships traveling through the Canal, rather than down the length of South America and rounding the treacherous waters of Cape Horn, reduced the length of the journey by almost 8,000 miles. The Canal cuts through 40 miles on the isthmus of Panama, using a series of locks to lift ships 26 meters above sea level into the more spacious confines of Gatun Lake, one of 17 man-made bodies of water used by ships. Another series of locks then lowers the ships back down to sea level. Today more than 14,000 ships pass through the canal each year, carrying more than 203 million tons of cargo.

When LST 357 reached the Pacific Ocean, it set its course for the islands of Hawaii. Along the way the ship's crew encountered some of the natural wonders that the sea has to offer. Halfway to Hawaii, some men, looking over the port bow, spotted a pod of whales, surfacing and blowing spouts of warm air that quickly turned to water vapor, rolling and diving with their giant tails flipping into the air and then descending into the depths of the sea. Another day, the men were called topside to the weather deck to see another natural wonder: flying fish. Delmar had heard talk of these winged creatures, but thought it nothing but a tall tale. Now he saw it for himself, these fish with pectoral fins large enough to enable the fish to take short gliding flights through air, above the surface of the water.

But this peaceful cruise and easy-going nature watching came to an end early the next morning, when, just after breakfast, the alarm sounded for battle stations. Instantly every sailor jumped into action and manned their designated positions. Fighter planes had been spotted approaching from the north, diving out of a bank of clouds and headed directly for the ship. Just as the gunnery officer was about to give the order to "Fire!" the ship's loudspeaker crackled with the command "Don't fire!" The planes had been identified as friendly. The loudspeaker continued, "Those three aircraft are U.S. Navy fighter planes and their pilots have just welcomed us to Hawaii and Pearl Harbor with the following news: JAPAN HAS JUST SURRENDERED, THE WAR IS OVER!"

It was August 14, 1945. Just hours later, LST 357 docked in the very place where the war had started almost four years earlier: Pearl Harbor. The great hulks of broken ships, bombed and burned on that day of infamy, still lay in the harbor. A small boat took Delmar and other sailors out to the USS Arizona, now a jagged wreck of steel and inside of which were entombed 1,177 men. Many of the men were weeping openly for their fallen comrades. Caught by surprise in the first minutes of the war, they were never given the chance to defend themselves or their country. Now Delmar felt tremendously moved by the sight, and the words "Remember Pearl Harbor" had a profound and eternal meaning for the ship's crew.

That evening, the whole city of Honolulu celebrated the end of the war—everyone, it seemed, except the crew of LST 357. The ship's skipper had cancelled all liberty, apparently concerned that nothing good could come of his crew joining a city-wide party. This was the second time that Delmar had missed a worldwide celebration. During V-E day (May 8, 1945), when the entire country and all of Europe had thronged and celebrated in the streets after the surrender of Germany, Delmar had been on board LST 357 at sea headed for dry docks in Jacksonville. Now, after a war that had started with the Japanese invasion of Manchuria in 1933 and had killed an estimated 50 million people worldwide, with the biggest celebration in the history of the world taking place, Delmar was stuck on a ship.

The next day, however, the crew was given liberty and allowed to visit the city of Honolulu, which Delmar found fascinating, the streets buzzing with activity. Some of the men went swimming in the Pacific Ocean in front of the Royal Hawaiian Hotel, a famous luxury hotel that the U.S. Navy had leased during the war to serve as a rest and recreation center for members of the Pacific Fleet. Other sailors attended theater shows featuring Hawaiian girls dancing in their grass skirts. Delmar bought a grass skirt for Helen and a beautiful white-on-white kimono for his mother.

Walking down a city sidewalk, Delmar noticed a large group of soldiers and sailors gathered around a large table, about five feet square. Delmar ventured over to see what the big attraction was about. Displayed on the table were hundreds of snapshots, and when Delmar took a closer look, he was surprised to find that they were photographs of hundreds of young women, of every possible size and shape, all naked as the day they were born. The merchant peddling this risqué material was doing a thriving business selling the erotic postcards to GIs, and about a month later, Delmar was to discover a reason for his success when a sailor started bragging immoderately about how pretty his wife was. When pressed to prove his point, the sailor proudly brought forth a snapshot, and Delmar instantly recognized that the sailor's would-be wife was actually one of those gals on the table in Honolulu. It turned out that three other sailors had the same picture for their sweethearts.

Since time immemorial, getting a tattoo has been a rite of passage for a sailor. The men of LST 357 were no different than their predecessors, though most of the sailors would get drunk before enduring the procedure in order to avoid feeling any pain. For Delmar, this was nothing less than being a sissy, and he told them so. Well, that did it. With their pride wounded, the offended sailors dared Delmar to get a tattoo without the benefit of inebriation. Somebody said, "I double dog dare you. You'll cry like a baby, Doc." Something about a dare always got Delmar pumped up to answer the challenge. It happened when someone dared him to go swimming in the Great Atlantic Hurricane of 1944, and it happened here again. "What's it worth to you to see me cry?" asked Delmar defiantly. Five men quickly put up ten dollars each. Fifty bucks was on the line. Delmar picked the smallest picture the tattoo artist had, a little robin, took off his shirt and pointed to a place on his right shoulder for the little bird to reside. Thirty minutes later, the work was done and not a tear was shed. Delmar put the five ten dollar bills in his pocket, then vowed he would never do that again. The pain had been excruciating. For the next few months, Delmar would suddenly take out a ten dollar bill, wave it in front of his buddies and exclaim, "But I didn't cry!" It always got a laugh.

The war was over, but the duties of LST 357 were not. Soon the ship was underway, taking a west by southwest course in a calm sea. The ship's destination was Kwajalein Island, part of the Marshall Island Group and the largest island in the Kwajalein Atoll, one of the world's largest coral reefs. When they arrived, Delmar was stunned and astonished by what he saw. As a boy of 11, Delmar had experienced a beautiful dream. He was standing in the wheelhouse of a large ship, looking out over the forecastle. As the ship approached land, Delmar walked toward the bow of the ship to catch a better view. Before him was a sight of unspeakable beauty: the island was filled with lush tropical trees—palm trees, banana trees, coconut trees—all bathed in a bright tropical almost heavenly light. He felt like he was looking at Paradise itself, and then he woke up. Now, 12 years later, here in the middle of the Pacific Ocean, thousands of miles from any land that Delmar had ever seen, he saw

154

his dream before him. Every detail matched his boyhood dream—the white coral sand, the beautiful tropical trees, the intensity and splendor of the tropical light. He had been here before! This was the island of his dreams! Being here was part of his destiny, part of a greater plan. He was so astonished that he spontaneously said out loud, "I've been here before." A shipmate who overheard the remark said dismissively "Doc, you're NUTS!"

Soon the ship pulled away from Delmar's mystical island, heading west to the island of Enewetak. Unlike most of the atolls in the area, which were lush and pristine with tropical growth, war had had its way on Enewetak. Years of bombing and shelling had reduced the island to a near lifeless sand bar, desolate and deserted except for one lone palm tree on the island's north end, from which swayed a single battered frond of green.

The ship continued westward on its journey, with calm seas beneath and a bright, blue nearly cloudless sky above. The next stop was Guam, and here Delmar received perhaps the most inspiring gift a young man who finds himself on the other side of the world from his family can receive: letters from home! There was one from Mother, one from Helen, even one from his brother Dave. Delmar read the letters so often that he thought he was going to wear out the words. The news was nothing eventful, ordinary communication about the weather, about who was doing what. But no matter what they had written, no matter how trivial or ordinary, it lifted Delmar's spirits.

The pressure was off. The deep but silent anxiety that stirs in the gut of every young man at war, caused by the unrelenting prospect that today might be the last day of your life, was gone, leaving a gentle and sweet peace. As for the future, there was no sense thinking about it until they got back home. All they had was the present moment—to seize, to enjoy. They filled the days with the games of youth. One day, it was announced there would be a swimming race, and the winner would receive a grand prize. Twenty sailors dove off the decks of LST 357 into the cool sparkling waters of the Pacific and raced 100 yards to a sister ship and then back.

Twenty sailors, kicking up white foam, their arms turning furiously, and leading the pack was Delmar. He had always been a strong swimmer, but when he won the race, the much publicized prize left him feeling disappointed. Four cases of beer was the last thing Delmar wanted after his run-in with alcohol in New Orleans. He hated the taste of the stuff (and still does today), so he gave all of it away to his more Bacchus-loving shipmates. They all thought he was absolutely nuts, but they sure enjoyed the beer.

After taking on supplies and refueling, the 357 headed northward and dropped anchor at Tinian Island. Delmar was unaware that his brother David had fought here in July 1944. Since that victory, the Seabees, the construction battalions of the U.S. Navy, had transformed the island into one of the largest naval air stations built during the war, with two B-29 airfields. Their second day there, the ship hauled up anchor, journeyed to the open north side of the island, and then turned back south into the inlet created by the atoll. A storm, which later developed into a typhoon, was approaching, and this cove was the safest place for the ships, protected on three sides by the curve of the island. The next day, the sea was relatively calm, but eight-foot swells were still rolling into the cove. Undaunted, some of the men went for a swim in the undulating sea. From the side of the ship, it was a 20-foot dive into the water, and like the famed cliff divers of Acapulco, the men had to time their jump with the incoming waves or risk scraping bottom in the shallow water. Inevitably, some of the men mistimed their dive, and with their skin scratched and clawed by the unforgiving coral shelf, they came to Delmar to patch them up.

The undertow was another danger lurking beneath the surface of the sea. Because the outgoing tides of the cove had only one exit point on the north side, the receding current could be violently strong. One sailor was sucked out by the undertow and disappeared. His fellow sailors dove and dove in vain to find him until they finally gave up the search. Two hours later, with the sea calmer, and the crashing of the waves less pronounced, they heard, a faint, weak voice calling from the sea. The missing sailor had survived the undertow, which had whisked him out about a half mile from the ship. Too weak to swim back, the sailor had found rest on an anchored buoy, climbing up a barnacled chain that severely scratched his belly, where he waited for rescuers to spot him or to hear his cries for help. He was one lucky sailor.

The next stop for the crew of the 357 was Saipan, just north of Tinian, the site of another island battle where his brother David had fought, and it seemed to Delmar that he could feel his brother's presence here in the shadow of Mount Tapochau, the 1,500-foot precipice at the center of the island that dominated the landscape. All around him, young Marines had died, and his brother had come face to face with the horror of war and seen its ugliness, just as he had on Omaha Beach.

Another swim party ensued to pass the hours, but this time it wasn't the undertow that rose out of the deep. A quarter mile off the island, the skipper had opened the bow doors and lowered the ramp into the water. The sailors fastened a large rope net to the end of the ramp, with heavy weights holding it down into the sea. The men dove off the ship and then a 4-knot current would carry them over to the net, where they would climb back onboard and dive again. They were like kids in a water park—diving and climbing over and over, when suddenly a shot rang out. The skipper had positioned a Gunner's Mate, equipped with a 30-06 rifle on each side of the ship to protect in case a shark came around. One did, and when the Gunner's Mate fired, the startled men quickly clamored aboard. The skipper said they could continue swimming if they wished, but somehow the festive atmosphere had been broken. No one returned to the water.

Swim parties were a popular activity after the war ended, but it wasn't all fun and games. The men onboard still had work to do and responsibilities to fulfill, and as a result, there was a constant supply of men who were sick or fatigued or injured for Delmar to take care of. Delmar's office was a small room, about eight feet by six feet, with one cot for the patient. There was also a small cabinet on top of which sat a rack, three feet by four feet, filled with the ointments, solutions and medicines that Delmar had concocted. He was essentially the ship's druggist, and no medicine could be administered without his approval. The office was also home to a spider monkey that Delmar kept as a pet. No one really knew how the animal had come to be part of the ship, but the homecoming did not last long. The spider monkey had a chain around his waist, and some of the men had taken to teasing the monkey by pulling the chain. Eventually, the spider monkey grew tired of this rough behavior and became vicious whenever anyone even appeared to be thinking about grabbing the chain. Delmar kept the monkey in his "Sick Bay" office whenever he was away or at mess. One day, he returned to find the medicine rack destroyed and all the bottles and vials broken and spilled on the floor. Hours and hours of Delmar's hard work lay in a heap on the floor. But Delmar took no revenge on the monkey. Instead, he took the spider monkey and set him free on the island of Saipan. Delmar knew he was happy to escape the ship and his imprisonment at the end of a chain.

As part of its mission, LST 357 picked up Army personnel and transported them to their new duty station. Soon, the ship was full of soldiers, and heavy equipment filled the tank deck. Fully loaded, LST 357 pulled up anchor and sailed out to sea on a north by northwest course toward Okinawa. Soon the ship encountered rough seas, and every "Mae West" life jacket on board was issued. Late that same afternoon, a solider reported to Sick Bay complaining of a sharp pain in his lower abdomen. He had all the classic symptoms of acute appendicitis, a condition requiring immediate emergency surgery. Delmar went straight to the skipper and apprised him of the situation. A radio dispatch went out requesting a sea plane be sent to transport the stricken sailor. No answer. Finally, a reply from the Admiralty Islands, 2,000 miles to the south, explained that no one could answer the call for help because a large and dangerous typhoon was just south of 357's position. At almost the same time, the skipper received an official warning regarding the dangerous storm and was told  to make all necessary preparations to ride it out. Admiralty Islands wished LST 357 Godspeed and signed off. The rough seas of that morning were now being whipped into a violent surge by gale-force winds. The typhoon was approaching swiftly.

Delmar went to work. Even without any official training, he was confident he could perform emergency appendectomy surgery, thanks to his operating room experience. But he also knew there was no way the surgery could be performed during the violent pitching and tumult of a full-blown typhoon. Surgery would have to wait. In the meantime, there was very real and impending possibility that the ship might sink in the storm. Precautions needed to be taken. Delmar tied the soldier into a wire stretcher, wrapped him in a blanket, packed him in ice. He then strapped two life jackets, the soldier's and his own, to the stretcher. To manage the pain, Delmar shot him full of as much morphine as he thought was safe. Then two soldiers helped Delmar carry the man up to the doorway just inside the radio shack and tied him to the bulkhead. In this position, the man was under cover and out of the ravages of the storm's wind and rain. But he was also stationed next to the outside door. If the call came to "Abandon ship," Delmar could quickly untie his patient, slip him overboard into the water and ride out the storm with him hanging on the stretcher. It was a desperate plan, but Delmar was facing a possibly desperate situation, and being a good swimmer, he had no doubt that the plan, if it came to that, would work.

As Delmar prepared his patient, the entire rest of the ship buzzed with activity as the crew frantically carried everything above deck that could not be tied down to the safety of the decks below. They "honeycombed" the top deck with ropes as an additional precaution to help keep sailors from being washed or blown overboard. The storm was a monster. Gusts of wind would suddenly hurl their force against ship, blowing it off course by 50 degrees. Sixty-foot swells, as tall as a six-story building, tossed the ship. To survive in a storm of this magnitude required great skill by the ship's skipper. If the ship was parallel to the incoming swales, the immense power of the wave would simply roll the ship over upside down and the vessel would sink to the bottom of the sea. Approach these mammoth walls of water at a 90-degree angle and the ship, straddling the top of the wave, with the bow and stern hanging in mid-air, would simply break in two. The only way to negotiate such a powerful storm was keep the ship's course at a 45-degree angle to the waves and pray that the wind would not whip the ship off course and that the pilot had the skill and experience to keep her true and steady. Fortunately, the skipper and his crew had the experience and the wisdom to make it safely through.

The storm lasted through the night, and Delmar was kept busy attending to the sick and the injured. He had to go to them; to ask these men to come to the Sick Bay was out of the question. He had swum in hurricane waters in Rhode Island, but Delmar knew this storm was deadly serious. Walking down the companionway, he would take one step and find himself with his left side lying against the wall as LST 357 was thrown to one side like a toy ship in a baby's bathtub. He would take another step and find himself in a near prone position, leaning against the right wall of the hallway. Just walking a few feet could take several minutes. It was slow going, and the storm lasted all night, pounding and pounding the vessel in an unremitting cauldron of water and wind that almost seemed malicious in its intent.

Dawn finally broke. The seas were calm. And no one had been killed or seriously injured. It had been a horrific night, and so shaken was the crew that no one showed up in the mess for breakfast. Just how lucky LST 357 was soon became apparent when two hours later, a troop ship that had broken in two was spotted. Only the rear half of the ship was afloat, and it was densely packed with anxious men. The skipper immediately radioed a distress call for help and received a prompt reply. Help would arrive in 30 minutes. Already carrying a maximum load of men and materials, LST 357 was unable to take on survivors and could only watch helplessly as it made its way to Okinawa. The Army soldier with the appendectomy still needed medical attention as quickly as possible and the ship radioed the base to have an ambulance standing by. The answer from the base was so garbled that Sparks, the radioman, couldn't make it out.

With Okinawa in sight, Delmar prepared his patient for transfer. But the ambulance never arrived. A quick glance inland revealed the reason. The typhoon had wrecked the base so extensively that it seemed it had been blown into the sea. With no other resources to turn to, Delmar immediately started taking inventory as to what he would need to perform the appendectomy. Then, glancing over the bow of the 357, he spied a more practical solution: a Navy Hospital Ship, fully equipped with the military's best surgical equipment and staff. Delmar rushed to his skipper. "Sir," he said, "would you please drop an LCVP (Landing Craft, Vehicle, Personnel) to send this patient over to that Hospital Ship?"

"Great idea," the skipper answered.

Delmar thanked the skipper and congratulated him for his fine seamanship during the storm. Soon he watched the LCVP roar away, taking the patient that Delmar had attended to for two days to the doctors who would save his life. Exhausted, Delmar went to his office to rest. For a while, at least, he had no one to take care of and no one to answer to. But that was soon to change.

Just before noon, Delmar awoke to a loud rap on his door and a voice barking out, "Doc, Skipper wants you in the radio shack *right now!*" Delmar walked into the radio room just in time to hear his skipper say in an abnormally nervous voice, "Yes sir, Admiral, here is the Pharmacist Mate right now." The skipper quickly handed the radio controls over to Delmar, who started to identify himself. But before he could even give his service number, Delmar found himself on the receiving end of a full-blown dress down by an admiral of the navy who was steaming hot. Delmar just listened and listened to the anger bellowing out of the receiver until he finally heard a question that got to the heart of the matter.

"Are you responsible for sending a U.S. soldier to a Naval Hospital Ship this morning?" asked the Admiral.

"Yes sir," Delmar answered calmly.

"Don't you know that you never send an army man to the Navy for medical treatment," barked the Admiral, still furious.

"Yes sir," replied Delmar.

"Well what have you got to say about that?" demanded the Admiral, as if his prosecution of Delmar had reached that critical question that would break the witness down.

Now Delmar knew it was correct military protocol for each branch of the military to treat its own wounded. But he also knew that in this specific case, following such protocol would have resulted in a dead soldier. But rather than making his case and possibly losing his temper, Delmar bit his tongue and made his point perfectly by asking one simple, direct question.

"How's the patient, sir?" he said.

There followed a long moment of dead silence. Finally, the Admiral responded in a defeated tone, "The patient had surgery at 08:30 and is now recovering. He will be fine. Over."

All Delmar could think to say was "Thank you, sir," but by that time, the Admiral was gone. Word spread like wildfire around the ship about Delmar Powell, with great respect and dignity, putting a wrong-headed Navy Admiral in his place. A great shout could be heard in the officer's quarters on the 357 that day. But by that time, Delmar was so tired that he was back in bed.

After docking and picking up troops at Okinawa, LST 357 headed for the island of Kyushu, the southernmost main island of Japan and home of the largest seaport in the world. On November 1, 1945, the ship landed on the beaches of Sasebo, Japan, at the southern end of the port. The bow doors opened, the ramp dropped down and one of the first group of occupational forces arrived in the nation of Japan. Soon, Delmar found himself walking the streets of Sasebo with two of his shipmates. Everywhere they walked, they received a cold reception. People looked at them with obvious disdain. Some stuck out their lips. Others would hiss at the sailors and spit towards them in a gesture of open hostility. The looks of hatred continued unabated until an old man and his wife beckoned to the sailors and then invited them into their house. Delighted at last to have found some sign of hospitality, the sailors agreed. They took off their shoes and entered the home. Their elderly male host turned out to be a retired Admiral in the Japanese Navy. He showed the sailors pictures of himself with government officials in Washington DC. The former Admiral had retired from the military long before the surprise attack on Pearl Harbor. As the couple served the sailors a traditional Japanese alcoholic drink made from rice, "sake" (one sip was enough for the abstemious Delmar), the sailors asked why the people of the city had been so unwelcoming, and the couple explained that the hatred for Americans was caused by the recent dropping of two atomic bombs on Hiroshima and Nagasaki that killed an estimated 140,000, the overwhelming majority of them being civilians, including women and children. The fact that the two atomic bombs had precluded the need for an invasion of the Japanese homeland, in which casualties would have easily exceeded 1,000,000, did not figure in the sentiments of the Japanese.

With the occupational troops and their supplies unloaded, LST 357 headed southward and again made port at Saipan. Like any physician, Delmar was always facing new medical challenges. One particular problem, a runny sore on the legs of several men, had not healed after a month of conventional treatment. Delmar asked "Sparky," the ship's radio operator to contact all the Naval vessels in the area and locate a Navy doctor to offer some advice. No Navy doctors were around. But about 30 minutes after the initial contact, an Army doctor said that his radioman had overheard the message, and he wanted to know if he could be of assistance. Delmar explained the medical condition, and the doctor invited him to come to his Army base, and they would work together on finding a solution. The next day, Delmar hitched a ride up Mount Tapochau with a jeep full of Marines. Two miles from the base, the Marines were taking another road, so they dropped Delmar off in a heavily wooded area and drove away. As Delmar started down the road, he came upon a sign that read, "DANGER JAPS." Every so often, as Delmar continued down the road, he would see another sign conveying the same warning. The war was officially over, but on Saipan and dozens of other islands across the Pacific, there were still Japanese soldiers who did not believe that the war was over or that their cause was lost—armed soldiers who were hiding in the thick, unsearchable jungle, waiting to ambush an American soldier. (Indeed, the last Japanese holdout was found in the Philippines in 1974.) Delmar walked quietly but with great haste to his destination. He felt an eerie mixture of anxiety and paranoia. It seemed that danger lay hidden behind every turn of the road, and he could not think of a more tragic fate than to be killed by a Japanese soldier *after* the war was over.

It was late afternoon now and the shadows of the woods were deeper and darker. Suddenly, Delmar felt startled by a single command, "HALT, who goes there?" When Delmar looked in the direction of the voice, he saw the barrel of a rifle pointed at his chest. Quickly Delmar blurted out, "Pharmacist Mate Powell from the ship U.S. LST 357." Keeping his guard up and the rifle still pointed squarely at Delmar's chest, the sentry barked back, "Advance and be recognized." Slowly Delmar walked toward the sentry and with great deliberation pulled out his dog tags so the sentry would realize, "Yes, this is an American soldier." When the sentry verified Delmar's identity, he dropped his guard and apologized for the rude welcome. He had been expecting Delmar, but he wasn't expecting him on foot, and just two days earlier, they had confronted two Japanese soldiers who were still fighting the war. Then the sentry smiled and welcomed Delmar to the base as he handed him a colorful card with a palm tree on the cover and poem on the inside:

> *Our Christmas trees are palms this year;*
> *Our snow is coral white,*
> *But our Yuletide greeting is the same,*
> *To bring you joy on Christmas night.*

"Merry Christmas, sailor," said the sentry with a smile. "The doctor is expecting you." It was Christmas! Christmas Day 1945! Surrounded by jungle greenery and balmy breezes, Delmar had not realized that today was December 25 until that very moment.

The Army doctor sent a jeep down to carry Delmar the rest of the way and invited him to a Christmas dinner with the other officers in the evening chow. After a festive meal, the doctor and Delmar walked a short way to the medical tent. The doctor said that he had a new drug, recently discovered, that had proven highly effective in recent reports. He showed Delmar a white powder and proceeded to demonstrate how to mix the powder into a salve. Delmar carefully wrote down the instructions and was ready to leave, eager to try out this new remedy on his long-suffering patients. Knowing that Delmar had walked the last two miles to camp and that the jungle still held the danger of Japanese soldiers who had not surrendered, the doctor arranged for Delmar to be driven back with a driver and two armed guards. The new drug the doctor had given Delmar was penicillin, and the sores that had festered for more than a month disappeared in short order as soon as Delmar applied the precisely calibrated salve.

Eventually, Delmar was transferred to a U.S. LCI-G-19 (Landing Craft Infantry, Gun). This small ship (100 feet in length with a 30-foot beam), one of the first landing craft used in the war, was old and beaten up. But Delmar didn't care. He had just been told that he had earned enough service points to be discharged from the Navy. He was going home. The trip back to America, however, was frustrating. LCI-G-19 was traveling with another equally ancient ship of the same classification. (Both ships would be decommissioned and "mothballed" as soon as they arrived back in the states.) The old motors on both of the ships just couldn't keep running for any extended period of time. When the engine on one of the ships shut down, the other ship would tie up and tow her for a while until her own engine died, and then the two ships would reverse roles. The little two-ship convoy was only making four or five knots an hour. But after days and days of this, and a brief stop in Hawaii, they limped into San Diego, a month later than planned. But all that didn't matter any more. After a six-day train trip, Delmar was back with his family in West Hartford.

Chapter Twenty-Eight

# Honors

## ~ David's Honors ~

1.  Legion of Merit: Awarded in 1969 for service in the National Emergency Command Post Afloat--part of the Office of the Joint Chiefs of Staff.

2.  Bronze Star with Combat "V": Awarded for service in Vietnam 1965-1966.

3.  Navy Commendation Medal with Combat "V": Awarded in 1945 for service on Iwo Jima. The Gold Star represents a second award of this decoration for moving elements of the 3D Marine Division to Vietnam in 1965.

4.  U.S. Army Commendation Medal: Awarded in 1958 for service in Lebanon.

5.  USMC Good Conduct Medal: Awarded in 1945 for four years honorable service as an enlisted man.

6.  American Defense Medal: Awarded for service in 1939 after Germany invaded Poland.

7.  American Theater Service Medal: Service 1942-1945.

8.  Asiatic, Pacific Theater Medal with Four Battle Stars: Roi-Namur, Saipan, Tinian, and Iwo Jima 1944 and 1945.

9.  WWII Victory Medal: 1945.

10. National Defense Service Medal: For service during Korean conflict. The Star is for a second award for service in Vietnam.

L to R David Dale, Harry Lee, with dad David

David at ceremony
where grandson Chip
recieved his Air Force wings

Kenneth R. Powell's Honors

(*Lto R*) The Air Medal, American Theater Medal, European Theater Medal,
Prisoner of War Medal, World War II Victory Medal

# ~ A Pilot's Return ~

When Kenneth returned to England to have a nostalgic visit to Deenethorpe, the old World War II air base where he had been stationed, he was met by Graham Bratley, a member of the 401st Bomb Group Society. This is a group of British men who want to keep the memory alive of the American fliers who were stationed in England. At the edge of the field at Deenethorpe, there is a monument of the 401st Bomb Group, and these British men maintain it and keep the grass mowed and place flowers. Graham took Kenneth on a tour of the few remaining buildings still standing. A photo was made of Ken standing in a field of wheat that had been the runway when the B-17's took off for bombing missions. Kenneth stood beside a door that was at the entrance of the building where the briefings took place as the crews were given their missions each morning.

As we walked by the fence to look at the monument, an elderly British couple who appeared to be near ninety years of age, approached our daughter and asked her if she knew someone who had been stationed there. Our daughter replied that her father was stationed there and was in the car nearby. The lady excitedly asked, "Can we meet him?" As they approached the car, the man walked slowly and feebly toward Kenneth. He raised his arms slowly and placed his hands on Kenneth's shoulders and stood silently looking at him for a few seconds. Looking directly into Kenneth's eyes, he said with great emotion, "You came and helped us." This experience on a dusty British country road where Kenneth had flown his B-17 bomber so many years ago made for him an indelible memory.

The members of the 401st Bombardment Group Historical Society continue to welcome veterans who return to Deenethorpe to visit. They host reunions, participate in ceremonies, preserve history, and maintain the monument commemorating the 401st Group.

# ~ Delmar's Honors ~

DELMAR STODDARD POWELL
CHART OF THE WORLD WAR II MEDALS EARNED

| ASIATIC - PACIFIC CAMPAIGN | AMERICAN CAMPAIGN | SEAL OF THE U.S. NAVY | WORLD WAR II CAMPAIGN | EUROPEAN _ AFRICAN MIDDLE _ EAST CAMPAIGN |

CAMPAIGN BARS

EUROPEAN - AFRICAN - MIDDLE EAST
With a bronze star for the battle of Normandy

WORLD WAR II      ASIATIC - PACIFIC      AMERICAN

SHIP NUMBERS AND NAMES ON WHICH DELMAR SERVED

U.S.S. L.S.T 357  U.S.S. L.S.T. 391      U.S. L.S.T. 508      U,S,S, ALBEMARLE      U.S.S. L.C.I. - G 19

| RIGHT SHOULDER PATCH | ASIA OCCUPATION SERVICE MEDAL | NORMANDY INVASION MEDAL | U.S. NAVY GOOD CONDUCT MEDAL | LEFT SHOULDER PATCH |
| U.S. NAVAL AMPHIBIOUS FORCE | | | | PHARMACIST MATE SECOND CLASS PhM 2/c |

DOG TAG ID
WORN ON A CHAIN AROUND THE NECK
DELMAR STODDARD POWELL
SERIAL NUMBER  642 64 81
BLOOD TYPE - A
USNR
(U.S. NAVAL RESERVE)

# ENLISTED RECORD AND REPORT OF SEPARATION
## HONORABLE DISCHARGE

85390

| 1. LAST NAME - FIRST NAME - MIDDLE INITIAL | 2. ARMY SERIAL NO. | 3. GRADE | 4. ARM OR SERVICE | 5. COMPONENT |
|---|---|---|---|---|
| Powell Roger E | 11 140 038 | Pvt | AC | AUS |

| 6. ORGANIZATION | 7. DATE OF SEPARATION | 8. PLACE OF SEPARATION |
|---|---|---|
| 3704th AAF Base Unit | 3 Nov 45 | Westover Field Mass |

| 9. PERMANENT ADDRESS FOR MAILING PURPOSES | 10. DATE OF BIRTH | 11. PLACE OF BIRTH |
|---|---|---|
| 42 Lancaster Rd W Hartford Conn | 22 Jun 26 | Grant Co Ind |

| 12. ADDRESS FROM WHICH EMPLOYMENT WILL BE SOUGHT | 13. COLOR EYES | 14. COLOR HAIR | 15. HEIGHT | 16. WEIGHT | 17. NO. DEPEND. |
|---|---|---|---|---|---|
| 42 Lancaster Rd W Hartford Conn | Blue | Brown | 5'10" | 160 LBS. | 0 |

| 18. RACE | | 19. MARITAL STATUS | 20. U.S. CITIZEN | | 21. CIVILIAN OCCUPATION AND NO. |
|---|---|---|---|---|---|
| WHITE X | NEGRO OTHER (specify) | SINGLE X | MARRIED OTHER (specify) | YES X | NO | Student O x |

## MILITARY HISTORY

| 22. DATE OF INDUCTION | 23. DATE OF ENLISTMENT | 24. DATE OF ENTRY INTO ACTIVE SERVICE | 25. PLACE OF ENTRY INTO SERVICE |
|---|---|---|---|
| | 25 Feb 44 | 27 Nov 44 | New Haven Conn |

| SELECTIVE SERVICE DATA | 26. REGISTERED YES | NO X | 27. LOCAL S.S. BOARD NO. | 28. COUNTY AND STATE | 29. HOME ADDRESS AT TIME OF ENTRY INTO SERVICE |
|---|---|---|---|---|---|
| | | | | | 236 Laurel St Hartford Conn |

| 30. MILITARY OCCUPATIONAL SPECIALTY AND NO. | 31. MILITARY QUALIFICATION AND DATE (i.e., infantry, aviation and marksmanship badges, etc.) |
|---|---|
| Ap & Eng Mech 747 | Sharpshooter |

| 32. BATTLES AND CAMPAIGNS | |
|---|---|
| None | Recorded: West Hartford, Conn. November 13, 1945 |

| 33. DECORATIONS AND CITATIONS | |
|---|---|
| None | Attest: |
| | Town Clerk |

| 34. WOUNDS RECEIVED IN ACTION |
|---|
| None |

| 35. LATEST IMMUNIZATION DATES | | | | 36. SERVICE OUTSIDE CONTINENTAL U.S. AND RETURN | | |
|---|---|---|---|---|---|---|
| SMALLPOX | TYPHOID | TETANUS | OTHER 28 May 45 C 28 May 45 Y 28 May 45 | DATE OF DEPARTURE | DESTINATION | DATE OF ARRIVAL |
| 15Dec44 | 28Dec44 | 26Jan45 | | None | None | None |

| 37. TOTAL LENGTH OF SERVICE | | | | | | 38. HIGHEST GRADE HELD |
|---|---|---|---|---|---|---|
| CONTINENTAL SERVICE | | | FOREIGN SERVICE | | | |
| YEARS | MONTHS | DAYS | YEARS | MONTHS | DAYS | |
| 0 | 11 | 5 | 0 | 0 | 0 | Pvt |

| 39. PRIOR SERVICE |
|---|
| None |

| 40. REASON AND AUTHORITY FOR SEPARATION |
|---|
| Convn of the Govt AR 615 365 Demobilization and Ltr WD GAP 220.8 19Sep45 |

| 41. SERVICE SCHOOLS ATTENDED | 42. EDUCATION (Years) | | |
|---|---|---|---|
| None | Grammar 8 | High School 3½ | College 0 |

## PAY DATA

| 43. LONGEVITY FOR PAY PURPOSES | | | 44. MUSTERING OUT PAY | | 45. SOLDIER DEPOSITS | 46. TRAVEL PAY | 47. TOTAL AMOUNT, NAME OF DISBURSING OFFICER |
|---|---|---|---|---|---|---|---|
| YEARS 1 | MONTHS 8 | DAYS 9 | TOTAL $200 | THIS PAYMENT $100 | | $ 3.45 | A W LENNAN LT COL AC 152.05 |

## INSURANCE NOTICE

IMPORTANT: IF PREMIUM IS NOT PAID WHEN DUE OR WITHIN THIRTY-ONE DAYS THEREAFTER, INSURANCE WILL LAPSE. MAKE CHECKS OR MONEY ORDERS PAYABLE TO THE TREASURER OF THE U. S. AND FORWARD TO COLLECTIONS SUBDIVISION, VETERANS ADMINISTRATION, WASHINGTON 25, D. C.

| 48. KIND OF INSURANCE | | | 49. HOW PAID | | | 50. Effective Date of Allotment Discontinuance | 51. Date of Next Premium Due (One month after 50) | 52. PREMIUM DUE EACH MONTH | 53. INTENTION OF VETERAN TO | | |
|---|---|---|---|---|---|---|---|---|---|---|
| Nat. Serv. X | U.S. Govt. | None | Allotment X | Direct to V. A. | | 31 Oct 45 | 30 Nov 45 | $ 6 40 | Continue 10000 | Continue Only | Discontinue |

| 54. [fingerprint] | 55. REMARKS (This space for completion of above items or other items specified in W.D. Directives) |
|---|---|
| RIGHT THUMB PRINT | Lapel Button Issued ERC 24Feb44 to 26 Nov 44 ASR Score 9 2 Sep 45 "This individual will be acceptable for further military service if presented for induction by Selective Service" |

APPLICATION FOR READJUSTMENT ALLOWANCES MADE THROUGH CONN. EMPLOYMENT SECURITY DIV. ON 2-18-46

| 56. SIGNATURE OF PERSON BEING SEPARATED | 57. PERSONNEL OFFICER (Type name, grade and organization - signature) |
|---|---|
| Roger E. Powell | ROBERT C HILLIARD Major Air Corps      Robert C Hilliard |

WD AGO FORM 53-55
1 November 1944

This form supersedes all previous editions of WD AGO Forms 53 and 55 for enlisted persons entitled to an Honorable Discharge, which will not be used after receipt of this revision.

35

175

## Chapter Twenty-Nine

# Forever Blue

The war was finally over. All four brothers were back home. The four stars in the window would stay forever blue.

Life moved on as inevitably as a river moves to the sea. The seven Powell siblings, as families almost always do, had gone their separate ways: getting married, starting families, developing careers. But on one splendid summer day in 1950, they were reunited. Eva Powell had organized the family reunion at Hartford's Elizabeth Park. The park's world-famous roses were in full bloom that day, thousands of them. Their bright soft colors dazzled the eye and a pungent scent hinted at the goodness and mercy that filled each of their hearts. For a moment, they were all together again. It was a moment they would cherish for all the days of their lives.

### ~ David ~

After being recalled to active duty for the Korean War, David decided to make a career with the Marine Corps. His service included a combat tour in Lebanon, a combat tour with his sons Harry and David Jr. in Viet Nam, assignment to the Naval War College, and duty aboard a Navy ship that served as backup floating White House in case of a nuclear attack during the Cold War. He retired as a Lieutenant Colonel in 1969 and settled in Florida.

He and his wife Martie had been married 56 years when, in 1995, David lost his battle with cancer.

David left behind 5 grandchildren and never got to meet his 6 great grandchildren.

Before he passed away, David attended the graduation of his first grandson, Harry J. Powell, from the United States Air Force Academy. The last time David wore his Marine Corps uniform was to commission his grandson in 1992. He had a new uniform made for the occasion and received a great deal of recognition at the Academy with many ribbons and medals. It was certainly a high point in his life.

## ~ Kenneth ~

Even before his discharge from the Army Air Corps, Kenneth had enrolled at Furman University to attend summer classes. There, while attending church, he met his wife, Kathy Owen. After obtaining a B.A. from Furman, Kenneth continued with his education, earning a B.F.A. from the Pratt Art Institute in New York, and M.Div. degree from Southern Seminary in Louisville, Kentucky. For the next 28 years, Kenneth utilized the remarkable mechanical and artistic skills he demonstrated in the German prison camp by working as an editorial artist at the Baptist Sunday School Board in Nashville. He retired in 1987. Kenneth is the father of four children—Kathyanne, Kenna, Kevin and Kara—and the proud grandfather of eight grandchildren.

## ~ Delmar ~

On June 14, 1947, Delmar married Helen Pye, the girl he met playing tennis in Elizabeth Park in the summer of 1945 before being sent to the Pacific Theater.

After the war, Delmar worked in a number of enterprises, eventually moving to Miami to work in the motion picture business. On March 23, 1958, Helen and Delmar became Christians, and for almost the next 50 years, Delmar followed his call to preach the Gospel around the world.

Delmar and Helen have one son, Gerry Elbridge (named after the only signer of the Declaration of Independence who is buried in Washington D.C.) and a daughter Penny Pye Powell Fryman. The son and daughter both live in Massillon, Ohio, with their families.

### ~ Roger ~

After the war, Roger attended the University of Miami, where he met his wife Arbutis Herman, better known as Dolly, during a tennis match. An art professor, impressed by Roger's artistic abilities, encouraged him to attend a good art school, and Roger enrolled at the Rhode Island School of Design in Providence. After graduating, Roger began his career as an architectural illustrator. He also continued his career as a fine-art painter, working out of his own studio, with Dolly assisting in all the work.

Dolly and Roger have four children. Roger II is a chief engineer for a design firm, Greg is a retired air traffic controller, and Gilbert owns a highly successful interior design firm. Tragically, their beautiful daughter Elizabeth was killed at the age of 21 by a drunk driver while working for Senator Claiborne Pell in Washington D.C.

Roger and Dolly have eleven grandchildren and three great-grandchildren. Roger has written three books, continues to paint and teaches at the Lighthouse Center for the Arts in Tequesta, Florida. You can see his work at www.rogpowell.com.

### ~ Harry ~

Always called "Junior," because he looked like his father, Harry D. Powell Jr. attended Providence (Rhode Island) Bible Institute in 1949 before transferring to the Moody Bible Institute in Chicago. There, he met a missionary who challenged Harry to work as a missionary in the jungles of Bolivia. Inspired by the challenge, Harry applied to the South America Mission and was accepted. While studying at Moody, Harry met Norma Hahn, and they were married in June 1954. Norma was accepted by the South America Mission in 1956, and shortly thereafter the couple began to raise money for their missionary work. In January 1958, they journeyed to Bolivia for their first term of service. After serving four years in Bolivia and 12 in Colombia, the couple returned to the United States, where they served in three pastorates. In March 1994, Harry succumbed to a lung disease with complications from viral pneumonia, leaving behind four sons and 21 grandchildren.

### ~ Kathleen ~

Always known as "Sis" by her brothers, Kathleen Oleva graduated from Hall High School in West Hartford and attended college for one year. She married her childhood sweetheart, John Goodhart. Kathleen went on to a successful career as a professional artist in fine-art watercolor, with her work displayed and sold in galleries across the United States.

After 55 years of marriage, Kathleen and John now reside in New Jersey. They have four children—Esther, John, Jimmy, and Karen—and eight grandchildren. John is an ordained minister of the Gospel of Jesus Christ, and the couple has served pastorates in Maine, Massachusetts, and New Jersey.

### ~ Billy ~

Joseph William Powell, the seventh and last child of Harry and Eva Powell, was born in 1935. At the age of 14, he gave his life to Jesus Christ. After completing high school in 1953, Billy graduated from the Moody Bible Institute in Chicago in 1956. He completed a B.A. and a B.D. from Gordon College in Massachusetts. While at Gordon he met Ellen Marie Bosworth, who was working on her R.N.

They both graduated from Gordon in 1962 and were married on September 8 of that year. They have four children: Lynn Ellen, J. William Jr., Nathan Todd, and Mark Alan. Ellen and Billy have had 45 years of marriage and ministry in Rhode Island, Massachusetts, New Hampshire, Illinois, and New Brunswick, Canada. Presently Billy is pastor of the Yacht Cove Community Church on Lake Murray in Columbia, South Carolina. In his own words, "Great have been my gleanings from the life, love and faith of my parents, each of my five brothers, and my one and only sister—with thanks to God!"

## Family Reunion
## Elizabeth Park Connecticut
## Spring 1950

| Harry | | Ken | Billy | Kathleen | Harry, Jr. | David |
| | Eva | David Dale | Martie | | Dolly | Delmar |
| | | Harry Lee | | Roger | | |

Ken              Delmar              Roger, Delmar, David